# *Another* RAGBAG OF RICHES

Collected by

JAMES CHILTON

With illustrations by Charlie Dunn

Also by James Chilton

*The Last Blue Mountain*
*A Ragbag of Riches*

A book that furnishes no quotations is no book, it is a plaything.

*Thomas Love Peacock (1785-1866), novelist, poet, satirist. Official of the East India Company*

Quotations are the gold mine of the human mind, the silver pearls of the wisdom ocean, and the cool drops of the rain of intelligence.

*Mehmet Murat Ildan (b 1965), Turkish poet, playwright and economist*

A quotation at the right moment is like bread to the famished.

*The Talmud*

The nicest thing about quotes is that they give us a nodding acquaintance with the originator, which is often socially impressive.

*Kenneth Williams (1926-1988), comedy actor*

I hate quotations. Tell me what you know.

*Ralph Waldo Emerson (1803-1882), American essayist, philosopher, poet*

# Contents

# Introduction

When *A Ragbag of Riches* was published in 2017, I never thought that a similar collection of quotations, quips, graffiti, newspaper correspondence, thoughts and advice – learned, humorous, thought provoking, sublime and trivial, could have been captured in four years: the entries of the original volume had taken many years to be swept up. Somehow, the eye and ear have been more attuned to catching deserving entries. In any case, here they are, a similar random collection – the essence of a commonplace book, but nevertheless arranged in sections that seem appropriate although many defy a label.

The introductory words of the previous Ragbag are still relevant as this volume explores much the same wordy landscape that seems to have successfully entertained. Perhaps there are now less prayers and poetry and the military has got its boots in but essentially it is a book for pleasure. So once again, I invite you to wallow or skip lightly through this melange, and mingle quiet music with amiable irreverence.

Chipping Norton
April 2021

For
Candida, Fenella, Sacha, Alexander

# 1 | The Human Condition

The cure for boredom is curiosity. There is no cure for curiosity.

*__Dorothy Parker__ (1893-1961), American poet, writer, humourist, political activist. Second marriage to Alan Campbell but kept name of first husband. Chosen epitaph 'Excuse my dust'*

Life isn't about dawdling to the grave, arriving safely in an attractive, wrinkle-free body, but rather an adventure that ends skidding in sideways, champagne in one hand, strawberries in the other, worn out and screaming "Yee haa, what a ride!"

*Written on a wall of The Mother Goose café in Bulls, New Zealand. Quoted from Music My Life by Brian Kay. Published 2020*

*School reports – reflections on youth:*

Edward is a charming boy, covered in mud, blood, ink and jam. I hope he never commits a murder because he is bound to be caught!

*__Oliver van Oss__ (1903-1992), a legendary Eton housemaster*

Rupert's handwriting is much improved this term. Alas only revealing a great deficiency in his spelling.

Works hard at the subjects he likes – needs to increase the number of subjects he likes.

Surely in a week you had time to write a shorter essay?

*Of Patrick Leigh Fermor, at The King's School, Canterbury:*
A dangerous mixture of sophistication and recklessness.

***Walter Sellar** (1898-1951), co-author of '1066 and All That', was a housemaster at Charterhouse. New boys were measured at the start and end of term and he was surprised to find that one boy had shrunk by half an inch. He began his report:* 'Henry has settled down nicely'.

***Kenneth Rose** (1924-2014), biographer, diarist and friend of royalty was for a short time a master at Eton. One of his students was Antony Armstrong-Jones and Rose wrote in his report:* 'Antony may be good at something but it is nothing we teach at Eton'.

---

*Correspondence in The Times in 2019 generated many examples of teachers' facetiousness:*

> The improvement in his handwriting has revealed his inability to spell.
>
> Give him a job and he will finish the tools.
>
> In rugby, Hobbs shows useful speed when he runs in the right direction.
>
> This boy has no need for a Scripture teacher. He needs a missionary.
>
> Unlike the poor, Graham is seldom with us.
>
> Fortunately, he has not lived up to his reputation.
>
> Although he visits the well of knowledge occasionally, he needs to go more often and with a bigger bucket.
>
> Sir, I write further to your letters on school sarcasm. During my brief teaching career I more than once wrote on a school report: 'Your son is trying.' It seemed to satisfy the parents just as it did me.

---

Having one child makes you a parent; having two you are a referee.

*Sir David Paradine Frost* (1939-2013), *television host, journalist, comedian, writer. Played for Nottingham Forest FC. Interviewed eight Prime Ministers and seven US Presidents*

Children aren't happy with nothing to ignore
And that's what parents were created for.

***Ogden Nash** (1902-1971), American poet*

Times are bad. Children no longer obey their parents, and everyone is writing a book.

***Marcus Tullius Cicero** (106-43 BC), Roman orator, statesman, lawyer, philosopher*

There's nothing wrong with teenagers that reasoning with them won't aggravate.

***Jean Kerr**, born Bridget Jean Collins, (1922-2003), Irish-American author and playwright*

Youth would be an ideal state if it came a little later in life.

***Herbert Asquith, 1st Earl of Oxford** (1852-1928), statesman, Prime Minister. Classical scholar. Alcoholic*

At 18 our convictions are hills from which we look; at 45 they are caves in which we hide.

***Francis Scott Fitzgerald** (1896-1940), American writer. Commissioned soldier. Alcoholic*

Education is what is left after what
you have learnt has been forgotten.

---

*Colette was once actually hailed in a London magazine – and quite seriously – as* 'The Queen of French Letters'.

*Sidonie-Gabrielle Colette (1873-1954), French author, actress, journalist*

*When Somerset Maugham lived in Cap d'Antibes, he invited his neighbour over to dinner who asked if he could bring Picasso, who was staying with him. Maugham's immediate answer was* 'Does he play bridge?'

***Somerset Maugham** (1874-1965), playwright, novelist, short story writer. Qualified as a doctor. Gay but married*

Summer bachelors, like summer breezes, are never as cool as they pretend to be.

***Nora Ephron** (1941-2012), American journalist, film maker. Three nominations for an Academy Award*

*Toutes les femmes sont comédiennes, à l'exception de quelques actrices.*
[All women act a part, save a few actresses.]

***Sacha Guitry** (1885-1957), French actor, director, playwright. Married five times, all to actresses*

*Five reasons why it's great to be a woman:*

1. You can put a duvet cover on a duvet without asphyxiating yourself.
2. You can observe a barbecue without feeling the urge to intervene.
3. You can wear a ponytail and not look like a total jerk.
4. You can wear women's underwear without being arrested.
5. You can remain silent whilst in a car with another female driver.

Being a woman is a terribly difficult task, since it consists principally in dealing with men.

***Joseph Conrad****, born Joseph Korzeniowski, (1857-1924), Polish/British novelist, sailor. Depressive*

What is love? I have met in the streets a very poor young man who was in love. His hat was old, his coat worn, the water passed through his shoes and the stars through his soul.

***Victor Hugo*** *(1802-1885), French poet, novelist and dramatist*

Let us have wine and women, mirth and laughter
Sermons and soda-water the day after.

***Baron Byron*** *(1788-1824), poet, politician and traveller*

'Conversation' is when three women stand in the corner talking. 'Gossip' is when one of them leaves.

***Herb Shriner*** *(1919-1970), American humourist*

I used to be Snow White,
but I drifted.

***Mary Jane 'Mae' West***
*(1893-1980),*
*American actress,*
*singer, playwright*

The British are suspicious of anything foreign but then they drive a German car to an Irish pub for a Belgian beer, then travel home, grabbing an Indian curry or a Turkish kebab on the way, to sit on Swedish furniture and watch American shows on a Japanese TV.

*Anon*

England has 42 religions and only two sauces.

***Voltaire,** born François-Marie Arouet, (1694-1778), French writer, historian, philosopher, poet. Critic of Roman Catholicism*

*Two views of heaven and hell:*

- Heaven is an English policeman, a French cook, a German engineer and Italian lover and everything organised by the Swiss.

  Hell is an English cook, a French engineer, a German policeman, a Swiss lover and everything organised by the Italians.

- Heaven is an English house with a Chinese cook, a Japanese wife on an American salary.

  Hell is a Japanese house with an English cook, an American wife on a Chinese salary.

An English army led by an Irish general; that might be a match for a French army led by an Italian general.

*George Bernard Shaw (1856-1950), Irish playwright, critic, political activist. 60 plays. Nobel Prize for Literature, 1925*

The Swiss are not a people so much as a neat, clean, quite solvent business.

*William Faulkner (1897-1962), American writer. Nobel Prize for Literature*

I hate Russian dolls, they're so full of themselves.

*Sathnam Sanghera (b 1976), British journalist. First in English from Cambridge. Fellow, Royal Society of Literature*

A lion goes into the Circus Maximus. The gladiator whispers into its ear, 'You've got to say a few words after dinner.' The lion slinks away.

If you kowtow too low, you show your arse.

*Anon*

They say the definition of ambivalence is watching your mother-in-law drive over a cliff in your new car.

*__David Mamet__ (b 1947), American playwright, film director, author. Pulitzer Prize winner*

When everything seems to be going against you, remember that the airplane takes off against the wind, not with it.

*__Henry Ford__ (1863-1947), American industrialist. Founder of Ford Motor Company*

Buy a pup and your money will buy
Love unflinching that cannot lie;
Perfect passion and worship fed
By a kick in the ribs or a pat on the head.
Nevertheless it is hardly fair
To risk your heart for a dog to tear.

*__Rudyard Kipling__ (1865-1936), journalist, poet, writer, novelist*

Be aware, a favourite has no friends.

*English proverb*

Princes are never without flatterers to seduce them; ambition to deprave them; and desires to corrupt them.

***Plato** (428-347 BC), Athenian philosopher*

In human affairs there is no certain truth and all our knowledge is but a woven web of guesses.

***Xenophanes** (570-475 BC), Greek philosopher, theologian, poet, traveller*

Against those who laud the present state of society, with its unjustly rich and its unjustly poor, with its palaces and its slums, its millionaires and its paupers, be it ours to proclaim that there is a higher ideal in life than that of being first in the race for wealth… Be it ours to declare that health, comfort, leisure, culture, plenty for every individual are far more desirable than the breathless struggle for existence, the furious trampling down of the weak by the strong, huge fortunes accumulated out of the toil of others, to be handed down to those who had done nothing to earn them.

***Annie Besant** (1847-1933), Irish women's rights activist, philanthropist, writer. Champion of human freedom. 300 books and pamphlets*

*Among Spike Milligan's bon mots is the aphorism that* 'All men are cremated equal'.

***'Spike' Milligan,** born Terence Alan Milligan (1918-2002), English/Irish comedian, writer, poet, actor. Early life in Rangoon, son of Captain Alphonse Milligan. Author of seven volume autobiography. One of the Goons.*

Money can't buy friends, but you can get a better class of enemy.

*Ibid*

There are no pleasures in life worth giving up for two more years in a care home in Weston-super-Mare.

*__Sir Kingsley Amis__ (1922-1995), novelist, poet, critic.*
*Twenty novels, six volumes of poetry. Booker Prize winner*

It is impossible to enjoy idling thoroughly unless one has plenty of work to do.

*__Jerome Klapka Jerome__ (1859-1927), humourist writer*

Loneliness is the poverty of self; solitude is the richness of self.

*__May Sarton,__ born Eleanore Sarton (1912-1995),*
*American/Belgian poet, novelist. Gay. 53 books*

Worry is like a rocking chair. It will give you something to do but it won't get you anywhere.

*Anon*

Success is having to worry about every damn thing in the world, except money.

***'Johnny' Cash** (1932-2003), American singer-songwriter, guitarist, actor, author*

Today is the tomorrow you worried about yesterday.

I highly recommend worrying. It is much more efficient than dieting.

***William Powell** (1892-1984), American actor. 96 films*

There are two kinds of statistics, the kind you look up and the kind you make up.

***Rex Stout** (1886-1975), American writer of detective stories. 'Best Mystery Writer of Century' – 1959*

*In the 20th century, the United States endured two world wars and other traumatic and expensive military conflicts; the Depression; a dozen or so recessions and financial panics; oil shocks; a flu epidemic; and the resignation of a disgraced president. Yet the Dow rose from 66 to 11,497.*

A man from the west will fight over three things: water, women and gold, and usually in that order.

***Barry Goldwater** (1909-1998), American politician, businessman, author. Senator and presidential nominee. Air Force major general*

*After the 1958 Revolution in Iraq, the sign in the Baghdad public swimming baths reading* 'NANNIES SIT HERE' *remained in place until 1973.*

I'd like to live like a poor man with lots of money.

***Pablo Picasso** (1881-1973), Spanish painter, sculptor, poet, stage designer.* Co-*founder of Cubism*

When someone says 'It's not about money', it's about money.

***Henry Mencken** (1880-1956), American journalist, satirist and scholar. Multi-volumed study on English language and hundreds of thousands of letters*

An income tax form is like a laundry list – either way you lose your shirt.

***John Sullivan,** known as **Fred Allen** (1894-1956), American comedian*

Saving is a very fine thing. Especially when your parents have done it for you.

***Sir Winston Churchill** (1874-1965)*

Too many people spend money they earned... To buy things they don't want... To impress people they don't like.

***William Rogers** (1879-1935), American actor, cowboy, humourist. Cherokee Indian*

You'd be surprised how much it costs to look this cheap.

***Dolly Parton** (b 1946), American singer, songwriter, guitarist, actress, author. Composer of 3000 songs*

I want a man who's kind and understanding. Is that too much to ask of a millionaire?

***Zsa Zsa Gabor** (1917-2016), American/Hungarian actress and socialite. Married nine times*

To attract men, I wear a perfume called 'New Car Interior'.

***Rita Rudner** (b 1953), American comedienne, writer and actress*

Men do cry, but only when assembling furniture.

*Ibid*

Dancing with her was like moving a piano.

***Ringgold 'Ring' Lardner** (1885-1933), American sports commentator and satirist*

I think women are foolish to pretend they are equal to men. They are far superior and always have been. Whatever you give a woman, she will make greater. If you give her sperm, she will give you a baby. If you give her a house, she will give you a home. If you give her groceries, she will give you a meal. If you give her a smile, she will give you her heart. She multiplies and enlarges what is given to her. So, if you give her any crap, be ready to receive a ton of shit!

*William Golding (1911-1993), British novelist, playwright and poet*

Erotic is when you use a feather.
Kinky is when you use the whole chicken.

*Live, laugh, love*
*If that doesn't work: Load, aim, fire!*

*Bumper sticker – Nevada, October 2019*

## LET'S DO IT

Adam and Eve did it originally.
Musicians do it with rhythm.
Prince Rainier did it with grace.
Students do it with tuition.
Workers do it laboriously.
Card players do it with patience.
Junkies do it at speed.
Anaesthetists do it generally.
The famous do it by repute.
Campanologists do it with appeal.
Magicians do it with illusion.
Alcoholics do it with spirit.
Criminals do it with intent.
Photographers are exposed when they do it.
Tricksters do it with confidence.
Underwriters do it with assurance.
Solicitors do it when instructed.
Barristers do it briefly.
Engineers do it with precision.
Charles had the dickens of a time doing it.
Insurance brokers do it with acclaim.
Dan did it daringly.
Bankers do it with interest.
Godot is still waiting to do it.
Publicans do it with licence.
Bank managers do it creditably.
Electricians do it shockingly.
Opticians do it out of sight.
Newsagents do it periodically.
Decorators do it with strippers.
Butchers do it beefily, and sometimes ham it up.
Speed cops do it with a siren.
Pile-drivers do it boringly.
Beer drinkers do it bitterly.
Dustbin men refuse to do it.

Postmen do it with an early delivery.
Poker players do it with a flush.
Some guys do it with a rope.
Physicists do it with energy.
Undergraduates do it to a certain degree.
Haematologists do it bloody well.
Some authors do it in a novel way.
Poets are well versed in it.
Reviewers do it critically.
Chilterns do it in their hundreds.
Smiths do it crisply.
Policemen do it with apprehension.
Psychologists do it mindfully.
Dentists are drilled to it.
Beauticians face up to it.
Broadcasters do it frequently.
Milkmen do it with the crème de la crème.
Mathematicians multiply when they do it.
Wykehamists do it mannerly
and carpenters screw it up.

*Maggie Chilton (b 1940), consultant psychotherapist, 1980*

**VIAGRA**

It might not make
you James Bond,
but it will make
you Roger Moore.

*Sign seen by the writer and broadcaster Gyles Brandreth (b 1948) at a chemist in Frome, Somerset*

I have outlived my usefulness,
So a quiet life for me.
Where once I used to scintillate
Now I sin 'till ten past three.
Where once I lived in CAPITALS,
My life intensely phallic,
Now I'm sadly lower case
With occasional *italic*.

***Roger McGough** (b 1937), poet, broadcaster, children's author, playwright. President of the Poetry Society, Fellow of Royal Society. Translator of Molière plays*

Out of work, divorced, usually pissed,
He aimed low in life and missed

*Ibid*

I'm at the stage in life when if a girl says 'No' to me I'm profoundly grateful.

***Heywood 'Woody' Allen**, born Allan Konigsberg (b 1935), American director, writer, actor, comedian. Four Academy Awards. Clarinet player*

The more I see of men the more I like dogs.

***Germaine de Staël-Holstein** (1766-1817), French historian and intellectual*

A clear conscience is usually the sign of a bad memory.

***Steven Wright** (b 1955), American comedian, actor, writer. Oscar and Emmy awards*

It has been my experience that folks who have no vices have very few virtues.

***Abraham Lincoln** (1809-1865), American Statesman and lawyer. 16th President of the United States. Assassinated 15th April 1865*

Do justice, love mercy and walk humbly with your god.

*Favourite quote of Rabbi Hugo Gryn (1930-1996). Survived Auschwitz. Mathematical scholar at Cambridge. Degrees in Hebrew. From Book of Michael*

*When Clive James first lived in London he had digs near Piccadilly Circus. Longing for an avocado as a reminder of home, he went to his nearest grocer – Fortnum & Mason. An elegant young man in a frock coat and striped trousers was pleased to help and offered a ripe fruit. James enquired how much it was and on being told it was ten shillings he exploded:* "There are so many that fall into my back yard that I have to sweep them up into a barrow. I tell you where you put that – right up your..." *The elegant young man held up his hand to stop him.* "Indeed sir, but unfortunately I'm already accommodating a pineapple at five guineas."

***Clive James**, born Vivian Leopold James (1939-2019), Australian critic, broadcaster, poet (nine published volumes). Fluent in seven languages*

The young man who has not wept is a savage, and the old man who will not laugh is a fool.

***Jorge de Santayana y Borrás** (1863-1952), Spanish poet, novelist, philosopher*

There are two types of people – those who do the work and those who take the credit. Try to be in the first group; there is less competition there.

***Indira Gandhi** (1917-1984), Indian politician, stateswoman. Twice Prime Minister of India*

I only know two tunes. One of them is 'Yankee Doodle' and the other isn't.

***Ulysses Grant** (1822-1885), American Union General. 18th President of the United States. Champion of African and Jewish contenders for political office*

If you think going to the moon is hard, try staying at home.

***Barbara Cernan**, wife of US astronaut Gene Cernan*

*Filling in an embarkation form on a channel crossing:*

*Harold Nicholson:* 'What age are you going to put, Osbert?'

*Osbert Sitwell:* 'What sex are you going to put, Harold?'

***Harold Nicholson** (1886-1968), diplomat, author, politician. Born Tehran. 3rd Class degree at Oxford. Married to Vita Sackville-West.*

***Osbert Sitwell**, 5th Baronet (1892-1969), writer, poet*

Work is where you go to escape your family.

***Janice Turner** (b 1964), journalist*

The brain is ill-equipped to comprehend the meaning of a nation that encompasses eleven time zones.

***Frederick Smith** (b 1944), founder and CEO FedEx. About Russia*

*Some mysteries of life:*

- How do you tell when you've run out of invisible ink?
- Why did kamikaze pilots wear helmets?
- If it's true that we're here to help others, what are the others here for?
- What is a free gift? Aren't all gifts free?
- What was the best thing before sliced bread?
- Why is there only one word for 'thesaurus'?
- Why is 'abbreviation' such a long word?

---

*Seaman Staines, Master Bates and Roger the cabin boy were legendary characters from the TV series Captain Pugwash. But in fact, the series' actual characters were Master mate, Toni the cabin boy and the pirates Barnabas and Willy.*

Middle age is when you are faced with two temptations and you choose the one that will get you home by 9 o'clock.

***Ronald Reagan** (1911-2004), 40th President of United States. Governor of California, sports commentator, Hollywood actor*

While looking for a needle in a haystack, you find the farmer's daughter

A lone shipwreck survivor on an uninhabited island managed to build a crude hut in which he placed all that he had saved from the sinking ship. One day he was horrified to find his hut in flames. It was the worst that could happen and he cursed God. Yet the very next day a ship arrived. 'We saw your smoke signal,' the captain said.

*Adapted from 'Guideposts', quoted by Walter A Heiby*

If I hear, I forget.
If I see, I remember.
If I do, I understand.

***Xun Kuang** (aka **Xunzi**) (314-217BC),*
*Chinese Confucian philosopher*

*The loss of confidence in the Greek economy which led to its sovereign debt crisis of 2007/8, spawned many articles of explanation. The 'Greek Problem' was neatly summarised by this apocryphal story:*

A tourist travelling through the country, gives a 100 euro note to the proprietor of a small hotel as a deposit for a room when he returns from visiting the north. The proprietor gives the note to the butcher to settle a bill for a side of pork and the butcher hands on the note to the farmer who supplied him a pig. The farmer hands on the note to the friend who lent him money for a holiday. The friend hands on the note to the prostitute who offered her services on credit and the prostitute hands the note to the hotel for the room she rented. When the tourist returns, the note is still in the hotel, no one has paid out any cash, no work has been done but all debts have been settled.

*Lunch, tea or dinner? Extracts from correspondence in The Times that stir the pot:*

> Mancunians and Lancastrians have tea – a cooked meal whether at five or eight.
>
> In Hampshire in 1950s 'elevenses' was 'lunch' to workers, who also had 'lunch' around three before going home for 'tea', which some called 'supper'. 'Dinner' was in the middle of the day. That would have been lunch for the elevenses brigade who might have had 'afternoon tea' or 'high tea' later.
>
> The difference between dinner and supper was that the former was provided or served by someone else.
>
> Look at the difference between ladies and ladies who lunch.
>
> In Norwich, a chip shop had three openings: Dinner, Tea and Supper.

***FE Smith, 1st Earl of Birkenhead*** *(1872-1930) and Lord High Chancellor, was known for his hard living and drinking. Addressing a meeting in Washington when drunk he noted the anxiety of his ambassador. Smith reassured him,* 'I'm good at tightrope walking' *he said; back came the reply* 'But only the rope should be tight'.

***Pope John*** **XXIII** *(1881-1963) on a visit to Argentina, was handed maté by a group of pilgrims. Warned by his security that this could be an imprisonable offence, he replied* 'It was only a group of pilgrims, not cardinals'.

*When asked by a journalist how many worked in the Vatican, after some thought, Pope John replied,* 'About half'.

*Known as The Good Pope, he was beatified in September 2000 and canonised in April 2014. He received the Presidential Medal of Freedom with the citation:* 'He brought to all citizens the sense of dignity of the individual, of the brotherhood of man and the common duty to build an environment of peace for all human kind'.

*In 2018, the Italian hamlet of Le Piastre opened a Museum of Lies. It includes:*

- Water from the Great Flood
- Hens' milk cheese
- The die cast by Caesar at the River Rubicon
- Christopher Columbus' plane ticket to New York

*On a trip to Canada, Brendan Behan was asked on television why he had come there. The writer replied:* 'Well, I was in a bar in Dublin and I saw a coaster which said 'Drink Canada Dry!' So I thought I'd give it a shot.'

***Brendan Behan** (1923-1964), Irish poet, novelist, playwright. Gaelic speaker*

Handing over the Hoover to my mother was like distributing highly sophisticated weapons to an underdeveloped African nation.

***Alan Bennett** (b 1934), playwright, actor, author. First class degree at Oxford. Fluent in Russian. Part of the Beyond the Fringe quartet*

The Internet is an élite organisation; most of the population of the world has never even made a phone call.

***Noam Chomsky** (b 1928), American linguist, philosopher, scientist, political activist. On the limitations of the World Wide Web, 1966*

Computers are like Old Testament gods; lots of rules and no mercy.

***Joseph Campbell** (1904-1987), American professor of literature*

*What gender is a computer?*

*A group of women concluded that computers should be referred to in the masculine gender because:*

1. In order to get their attention, you have to turn them on.
2. They have a lot of data but are still clueless.
3. They are supposed to help you solve your problems, but half the time they are the problem.
4. As soon as you commit to one, you realise that, if you had waited a little longer, you could have had a better model.

*Men, on the other hand, decided that computers should definitely be referred to in the feminine gender because:*

1. No one but themselves understands their logic.
2. The native language they use to communicate with other computers is incomprehensible to everyone else.
3. Even your smallest mistakes are stored in their long-term memory for later retrieval.
4. As soon as you make a commitment to one, you find yourself spending half your pay on accessories for it.

---

Only two things are infinite. The universe and human stupidity. And I'm not sure about the universe.

***Albert Einstein** (1879-1955), German theoretical physicist. Violinist*

When asked if they were well known, the president of The Flat Earth Society replied that they were known round the world.

*International Flat Earth Society was formed in 1956 in Dover (a successor to Universal Zetetic Society). Believers in Biblical literalist theology. 'The earth is flat because the Bible says it is.' Humanity lives on a disc with the North Pole at its centre and a 50-foot-high wall of ice around it.*

The road of life is paved with flat squirrels who couldn't make a decision.

Tradition is tending the flame, not worshipping the ashes.

***Gustav Mahler** (1860-1911), Austrian composer. Director Vienna Court Opera, New York Philharmonic, Metropolitan Opera*

There is nothing more to happiness than good health and a short memory.

***Albert Schweitzer** (1875-1965), Alsatian theologian, organist, writer, philosopher, physician. Nobel Prize for Peace*

One of the keys to happiness is a bad memory.

*__Rita Mae Brown__ (b 1944), American writer, feminist activist. One-time lover of Martina Navratilova*

Life is rather like a tin of sardines – we are all looking for the key.

*__Alan Bennett__ (b 1934), playwright, screenwriter, actor, author. Medievalist at Oxford*

Intelligence without ambition is a bird without wings.

*__Salvador Dalí, Marquis of Dalí de Púbal__ (1904-1989), Spanish surrealist*

There is no education like adversity.

*__Benjamin Disraeli, 1st Earl of Beaconsfield__ (1804-1881), politician, twice Prime Minister, novelist*

So remember that a good conversationalist is, first and foremost, a good listener. In fact, among people who are widely regarded as great conversationalists, there are some who hardly ever open their mouths at all.

*__Quentin Crisp__, born Denis Pratt (1908-1999), effeminate writer, actor, cross-dresser*

Euphemisms are unpleasant truths wearing diplomatic cologne.

*Ibid*

A bore is a man who, when you ask him how he is, tells you.

*__Ambrose Bierce__ (1842-1914), American writer, journalist, poet. Travelling to Mexico, he was never seen again*

Judge a man by his questions rather than by his answers.

*__Voltaire,__ born François-Marie Arouet (1694-1778), French writer, historian, wit, philosopher. Wrote 2000 books. Fluent in English, Italian, Spanish*

Human speech is like a cracked kettle on which we tap crude rhythms for bears to dance to, while we long to make music that will melt the stars.

*__Gustave Flaubert__ (1821-1880), French novelist*

They don't make men like they used to.

*__Marie Colvin__ (1956-2012), British/American foreign correspondent. In September 1999, the only journalist left in Dili, East Timor*

*Sydney Smith about Lord Macaulay:*

He has occasional flashes of silence that make his conversation perfectly delightful.

***Thomas Babington Macaulay, 1st Baron Macaulay*** *(1800-1859), historian, politician*

***Sydney Smith*** *(1764-1840), admiral, served in American and French revolutions*

Blessed are the cracked, for they shall let in the light.

***'Groucho' Julius Marx*** *(1890-1977), American comedian and writer*

If you are ever attacked in the street do not shout 'Help!', shout 'Fire!' People adore fires and always come rushing. Nobody will come if you shout 'help'.

***Jean Barker, Baroness Trumpington*** *(1922-2018), politician. Fluent in French, German and Italian. Worked at Bletchley Park*

The Conservative Party is a generous party. It always forgives those who are wrong. Sometimes it even forgives those who are right.

***Iain Macleod*** *(1913-1970), politician and cabinet minister. Winner of Bridge Gold Cup*

In the United States you run for office.
In the United Kingdom you stand for office.

There's no situation so bad that it can't get worse tomorrow.

***Damian Green*** *(b 1956), politician*

Show me a hero and I will write you a tragedy.

***Francis Scott Fitzgerald** (1896-1940), American writer. Alcoholic*

*In 1842* ***Oliver Wendell Holmes*** *described homeopathy as* 'a mingled mass of perverse ingenuity, of tinsel erudition, of imbecile credulity and of artful misrepresentation'. *He hoped that soon it would be sleeping in the grave of oblivion along with the Royal Touch for scrofula, Bishop Berkeley's tar-water, and Dr Perkin's Metallic Tractors. He was wrong.*

Nothing changes. I despair.

***Hugh Pennington** (b 1938), Emeritus Professor of Bacteriology, Aberdeen University*

To err is human – but it feels divine.

***Mae West** (born Mary Jane West) (1893-1980), American actress, singer, comedienne, sex symbol. Starred in 18 Broadway plays and 12 films.*

I wanted your soft verges, but you gave me your cold shoulder.

***Adrian Henri** (1932-2000), poet and painter*

One failure on top of another.

***AR Ammons** (1926-2001), American poet. From 'Their Sex Life'*

The only time a woman really succeeds in changing a man is when he's a baby.

***Natalie Wood** (born Natalia Nikolaevena Zakharenko) (1938-1981), American film actress. Three Academy awards, four Golden Globes.*

## HYMN OF AN IMMIGRANT

I come to England poor and broke
Go on dole, see Labour bloke
Fill in forms, have lots of chatters
Kind man give me lots of ackers.
I thank him much and then he say,
Come next week and get more pay
You come here we make you wealthy
Doctor too, to make you healthy
Six months on dole, get plenty money
Good 'Pal' meat to fill my tummy
Send for friends from Pakistan
Tell them come as quick as can
Plenty of us on the dole
Lovely suit and big bank roll
National Assistance is a boon
All the darkies on it soon
They come in rags and tatters
Go on dole and get some ackers
Then come with me and live together
One bad thing, the bloody weather
One day white man come inside
Ask me if I wash in Tide
I say, yes, we wash in Tide
Too damn cold to wash out-tide
All get nicely settled down
Fine big house in busy town
Fourteen families living up
Fourteen families down
All are paying nice big rent
More in garden... live in tent
Soon I send for wife and kids
They won't have to live in digs
Six months later big bank roll
Still go Labour... draw more dole
Wife gets glasses... teeth and pills
All are free, we get no bills.
White man says he pays all year
To keep National Assistance here
Bless all white men big and small
For paying tax to keep us all.
We think England damn good place
Too damn good for white man's race
If he not like coloured man
Plenty room in Pakistan.

# 2 | Love, Marriage, Home and the Family

Better to have an old man to humour, than a young rake to break your heart.

***Thomas Fuller** (1608-1661), clergyman and historian*

Husbands are like fires. They go out when unattended.

***Zsa Zsa Gabor** (born Sari Gabor) (1917-2016), Hungarian/American actress and socialite. Nine husbands, one child, ten adopted sons*

We had a lot in common. I loved him and he loved him.

***Shelley Winters** (born Shirley Schrift) (1920-2006), American film actress. Two Academy Awards. 135 films*

I want my children to have all the things I couldn't afford. Then I want to move in with them.

***Phyllis Diller** (1917-2012), American comedienne, actress, artist and pianist*

Never marry for money. Divorce for money.

***Wendy Liebman** (b 1961), American comedienne and psychologist*

The reason why Englishmen are the best husbands in the world is because they want to be faithful. A Frenchman or an Italian will wake up in the morning and wonder what girl he will meet. An Englishman wakes up and wonders what the cricket score is.

***Dame Barbara Cartland** (1901-2000), prolific romantic novelist. 723 novels translated into 38 languages*

When a man brings his wife flowers for no reason – there's a reason.

***Molly McGee***

Keep your tents separate but bring your hearts together.

*Arab proverb*

Don't get mad, get everything.

***Nana 'Ivanka' Trump** (b 1981), American business woman and author. Second child of President Trump*

*Husband:* 'What would you like for Christmas?'
*Wife:* 'A divorce.'
*Husband:* 'I wasn't thinking of spending that much.'

A good marriage lasts for ever. A bad one just seems to.

*Anon*

The only thing I really mind about going to prison is the thought of Lord Longford coming to visit me.

***Richard Ingrams** (b 1937), journalist.*
*Founder of 'Private Eye' and 'The Oldie'*

The best time to make friends is before you need them.

***Ethel Barrymore** (born Ethel Blythe) (1879-1959),*
*American actress of stage and screen*

When I was 17 my dearest wish was to be a writer. Now I am a writer my dearest wish is to be 17.

***Denis Norden** (1922-2018), comedy writer and television*
*presenter. Could recite Hamlet by heart*

It's a funny kind of month, October. For the really keen cricket fan, it's when you discovered that your wife left you in May.

*Ibid*

Many people walk in and out of your life, but only true friends leave their footprints on your heart.

***Eleanor Roosevelt** (1884-1962), First Lady to President Roosevelt*
*during his four terms in office. Activist for womens' rights*

We will go tandem as man and wife
'Peddling' away down the road of life.
You'll take the load in each trip we take;
If I don't do well you can use the brake

*__Katie Lawrence__ (1868-1913), music hall singer.*
*From 'Daisy Bell: A Bicycle Made for Two'.*
*Painted 162 times by Walter Sickert*

Love is like a tree: it grows by itself, roots itself deeply in our being and continues to flourish over a heart in ruin. The inexplicable fact is that the blinder it is, the more tenacious it is. It is never stronger than when it is completely unreasonable.

*__Victor Hugo__ (1802-1885), French novelist, poet and dramatist. Artist of 4,000 drawings*

Day's fondest moments are at dawn,
Refreshed by his long sleep, the Light
Kisses the languid lips of Night
Ere she can rise and hasten on.
All glowing from his dreamless rest
He holds her closely to his breast,
And sees her dusky eyes grow dim,
Till lo! she dies for love of him.

*__Ella Wilcox__ (1850-1919), American poet and author*

At first we want life to be romantic; later to be bearable;
finally, to be understandable.

*__Louise Bogan__ (1897-1970), American poet*

There's only one way to handle a woman – but no one knows what it is.

What greater thing is there for two human souls than to feel that they are joined for life, to strengthen each other in all labour, to rest on each other in all sorrow, to minister to each other in all pain and to be with each other in silent unspeakable memories.

*__Mary Ann Evans__, pen name __George Eliot__, (1819-1880), novelist, poet, translator. Her novel 'Middlemarch' voted tenth greatest literary work ever written*

Feet, why do I need them if I have wings to fly?

*__Frida Kahlo__ (1907-1954), Mexican artist. In her diary after the amputation of her right leg (1953).*

I tried to drown my sorrows, but the bastards learnt how to swim.

*ibid*

# 3 | Travel

If you look like your passport photograph, you probably need the journey.

*Harvey Earl Wilson (1907-1987), American columnist*

If you don't know where you are going, you'll end up someplace else.

*Lawrence 'Yogi' Berra (1925-2015), professional basketballer with Yonkers*

Too often travel, instead of broadening the mind, merely lengthens the conversation.

*Elisabeth Drew (b 1935), American political journalist*

Travel broadens the behind.

***Stephen Fry** (b 1957), actor, writer and comedian*

It is said that travel broadens the mind; but you must have the mind.

*Gilbert Chesterton, known as **GK Chesterton** (1874-1936), writer, philosopher, theologian, artist and critic – the 'Prince of Paradox'. Graduate of Slade School of Art. Author of 80 published books*

There is no greater bore than the travel bore.

***Victoria Sackville-West** (1892-1962), poet, novelist, gardener, designer. Vietch Memorial Prize. Chatelaine of Sissinghurst*

Never go abroad; it's a dreadful place.

***King George V** (1865-1936)*

I don't hold with abroad and think that foreigners speak English when our backs are turned.

***Quentin Crisp** (born Denis Pratt) (1908-1999), writer, actor, professional model*

We had a very successful trip to Russia – we got back.

***Bob Hope** (born Leslie Townes Hope) (1903-2003), British/American actor, comedian, dancer, athlete, author. Five Academy Awards. 100 years old*

The average tourist wants to go places where there are no tourists.

***Sam Ewing** (b 1949)*

It's a place where 100 roubles is not money, 1,000 kilometres is no distance, and half a bottle of vodka is no drink.

***Eric Newby*** *(1919-2006), travel author. War hero, later in family fashion business. Describing the Soviet Union*

The worst thing about being a tourist is having other tourists recognize you as a tourist.

***Russell Baker*** *(1925-2019), American former columnist for The New York Times. Two Pulitzer Prizes. Librettist*

The scientific theory I like best is that the rings of Saturn are composed entirely of lost airline baggage.

***Mark Russell*** *(b 1932), American comedian and political satirist*

In Milan traffic lights are instructions. In Rome they are suggestions. In Naples they are Christmas decorations.

***Antonio Martino*** *(b 1942), Italian politician. Professor of Economics*

Sir, I was amused to read Matthew Dick's account of red traffic lights in Italy. In the same vein, the Maltese transport minister was once interviewed on the radio and was asked why road traffic accidents were so common in Malta. 'Well,' he replied, 'in Britain they drive on the left, in Europe they drive on the right, but here in Malta we drive in the shade.'

*The Times*

It is peculiar that all the sights in Rome are called after London cinemas.

***Nancy Mitford*** *(1904-1973), novelist, biographer, journalist. Originator of 'U' and 'non-U'. Eldest of six Mitford daughters*

Traditionally, in France, the most esteemed member of society is the woman. In England it's the horse.

*Flora Tristan (1803-1844), French/Peruvian socialist writer on women's struggles*

A kiss on the cheek is sufficient greeting. After all, we are not all French generals.

***Lady Diana Cooper****, Viscountess Norwich (1892-1986), socialite, aristocrat, actress. Founder of the intellectual group The Coterie. Editor and writer*

Stop worrying about the potholes, just enjoy the journey.

***Barbara Hoffman*** *(b 1931), Star of All-American Girls Professional Baseball League*

What a classy hotel! The towels were so thick and fluffy I could hardly close my suitcase.

*Anon*

The hotel was enormous – to call the front desk you had to call long-distance.

*Anon*

*During the '30s, the Waldorf Hotel, New York was the most luxurious hotel of its time. The poet Wallace Stevens wrote of it:*

You touch the hotel the way you touch moonlight

***Wallace Stevens** (1879-1955), American poet and lawyer*

He who returns from a journey is not the same as he who left.

*Chinese proverb*

We wander for distraction, but we travel for fulfilment.

*Anon*

I hold that it is the duty of a man to see other lands but love his own.

***Edward Verrall Lucas** (1868-1938), essayist, playwright, poet, humourist and biographer*

When it comes to flying, I am a nervous passenger but a confident drinker.

***Martin Amis** (b 1949), novelist and screenwriter. Professor of Creative Writing at Manchester University. First in English at Oxford. Editor, New Statesman*

May the fleas of a thousand camels infest your armpits.

*Arab curse*

I refuse to travel on any airline where the pilots believe in reincarnation.

***Spalding Gray** (1941-2004), American actor. Committed suicide by jumping off Staten Island Ferry*

The world is a curious sight and very much unlike what people write.

***George Byron, 6th Baron Byron** (1788-1824), poet, politician and traveller*

As you travel, take only pictures, cast only shadows, leave only ripples of understanding.

***David Bellamy** (1933-2019), botanist, television presenter and environmental campaigner*

A good traveller leaves no track or trace.

***Lao Tzu** (6th century – 4th century BC), philosopher, in the Tao Te Ching*

*In a letter to the station master at Baker Street:*

Sir, Saturday morning, although occurring regularly, always seems to take this railway by surprise.

***Sir William Schwenck Gilbert** (1836-1911), dramatist, librettist, illustrator. Collaborator with Arthur Sullivan in 14 comic operas. Eighty dramatic works. Built Garrick theatre*

**Beneath this slab**
**John Brown is stowed.**
**He watched the ads**
**And not the road.**

***Ogden Nash** (1902-1971), American poet*

Ah, what is more blessed than to put care aside, when the mind lays down its burden, and spent with distant travel, we come home again and rest on the couch we long for.

***Gaius Catullus** (c84-c54 BC), Roman poet*

Travel they say improves the mind,
An irritating platitude
Which frankly, *entre nous*,
Is very far from true.

***Sir Noël Coward** (1899-1973), playwright, composer, director, singer, lyricist*

In an underdeveloped country, don't drink the water; in a developed country, don't breathe the air.

*__Jonathan Raban__ (b 1942), novelist, travel writer*

Remember that a foreign country is not designed to make you comfortable. It is only designed to make its own people comfortable.

*__Clifton 'Kip' Fadiman__ (1904-1999), American intellectual, author, editor, television personality and translator*

To live in Australia permanently is rather like going to a party and dancing all night with your mother.

*__Barry Humphries__ (b 1934), Australian comedian, actor and satirist. Originator of Dame Edna Everage and Sir Les Patterson*

No man needs a vacation so much as the person who has just had one.

*__Elbert Hubbard__ (1856-1915), American publisher, writer, salesman and philosopher*

It is amazing how nice people are to you when they know you are going away.

*__Michael Arlen,__ born Dikran Kouyoumdjian (1895-1956), Armenian essayist, short story writer, novelist and playwright*

The fool wanders, the wise man travels.

*Anon*

The roads are steep and dangerous, the wind bitingly cold, fierce dragons frequently molest travellers with inflictions. Those who travel this road should not wear red nor carry loud calabashes.

***Hsuan Tsang** (602-664), Chinese Buddhist pilgrim and traveller. Scholar and translator. Known for 17-year journey in India*

Of the gladdest moments in human life, methinks, is the departure upon a distant journey into unknown lands. Shaking off with one mighty effort the fetters of Habit, the leaden weight of Routine, the cloak of many Cares and the slavery of Civilization, man feels once more happy.

***Sir Richard Burton** (1821-1890), explorer, translator, writer, soldier, spy, poet, diplomat. Reputedly spoke 25 languages*

It was a strange, wild scene. The black basaltic field was dotted with the huge and doubtful forms of spongy-footed camels, with silent tread, looming like phantoms in the midnight air; the hot wind moaned, and whirled from the torches flakes and sheets of flame and fiery smoke; whilst ever and anon a swift-travelling Takhtrawan, drawn by mules, and surrounded by runners bearing gigantic cressets, threw a passing glow of red light upon the dark road and the dusky multitude.

*Ibid*

The wish to travel seems to me characteristically human: the desire to move, to satisfy your curiosity or ease your fears, to change the circumstances of your life, to be a stranger, to make a friend, to experience an exotic landscape, to risk the unknown.

***Paul Theroux** (b 1941), American novelist and travel writer*

There in the mist, enormous, majestic, silent and terrible, stood the Great Wall of China. Solitarily, with the indifference of nature herself, it crept up the mountain side and slipped down to the depth of the valley. Menacingly, the grim watch-towers, stark and foursquare, at due intervals stood at their posts. Ruthlessly, for it was built at the cost of a million lives and each one of those great grey stones has been stained with the bloody tears of the captive and the outcast, it forged its dark way through a sea of rugged mountains. Fearlessly it went on its endless journey, league upon league to the farthermost regions of Asia, in utter solitude, mysterious like the great empire it guarded.

***Somerset Maugham** (1874-1965), novelist, playwright, short story writer. Spy. Bisexual. 51 film adaptations, ten novels, numerous stories. 'On a Chinese Screen', 1922*

*Language:*

*The English language has four times as many words as the French language.*

*Only the English words abstemious and facetious contain all five vowels in alphabetical order.*

My wife is teaching me Cuban. It's like Spanish but with fewer words for luxury goods.

***Emo Philips** (b 1956), American comedian, actor*

Is there anything worse than speaking a foreign language to someone who turns out to be English.

***Michael Frayn** (b 1933), playwright and novelist, journalist. Russian translator*

There's a store in New York called Bonjour Croissant. It makes me want to go to Paris and open a store called Hello Toast.

*Frances Lebowitz (b 1950), American satirist and actor. Social commentator*

In Istanbul I was known as 'English Delight'.

***Noël Coward***

He mobilized the English language and sent it into battle to steady his fellow countrymen and hearten those Europeans upon whom the long dark night of tyranny had descended.

*Ed Murrow (1908-1965), American broadcaster. On Churchill's 80th birthday, 30 November*

# 4 | Creativity: the arts, literature, music and film

All newspaper editorial writers ever do is come down from the hills after the battle is over and shoot the wounded.

*Anon*

He was like a man who had woken too early in the darkness when everyone else was still asleep.

***Dimitri Mereshkovsky** (1866-1941), Russian poet, novelist and critic. Nine nominations for Nobel Prize.*

*When David Bowie auditioned for the BBC in 1965 at the age of 18, he performed three songs with his group The Lower Third for the Talent Selection Group. The panel, which had to approve every act hoping to be played on BBC radio, was unimpressed by their repertoire, which included a cover of Chim Chim Cher-ee from Mary Poppins. One judge declared that* 'The singer is a cockney type but not outstanding enough'. *Another dismissed Bowie as an* 'amateur-sounding vocalist who sings wrong notes and out of tune. A singer devoid of personality.'

*David Bowie, (born David Jones) (1947-2016), influential singer-songwriter. Changed name to that of the American pioneer James Bowie and his bowie knife. Married to Iman. Sold 100m records. Winner of five Grammy Awards*

I don't know anything about music. In my line you don't have to.

*Elvis Presley (1935-1977), American singer and actor, musician and sex symbol. Record sales of over 600m*

'Can't act, slightly bald; can dance a little.' *An RKO Radio report of Fred Astaire's first screen test. Followed up by a memo:* 'In spite of his enormous ears and bad chin line, he has tremendous charm...'

*Fred Astaire (1899-1987), American dancer, singer, actor, choreographer. 31 musical films, ten Broadway musicals. Successful racehorse breeder; skateboarder*

*Lines I wish I had written:*

The Duke's moustache was rising and falling like seaweed on an ebb tide.

The swan made a hissing noise like a tyre bursting in a nest of cobras.

I could see that if not actually disgruntled, he was far from being gruntled, so I tactfully changed the subject.

It was one of those still evenings you get in the summer, when you can hear a snail clear its throat a mile away.

*The real name of music hall entertainer and TV personality Bud Flanagan (1896-1968) was Chaim Ruben Weintrop. He changed his name to that of the sergeant who brutalised him in the army, as catharsis.*

That he was a coxcomb and a bore, weak, vain, pushing, curious, garrulous, was obvious to all who were acquainted with him. That he could not reason, that he had no wit, no humour, no eloquence, is apparent from his writings. Nature had made him a slave and an idolater. His mind resembled those creepers which botanists call parasites and which can subsist only by clinging round the stems and imbibing the juices of stronger plants.

Servile and impertinent, shallow and pedantic, a bigot and a sot, bloated with family pride, eternally blustering about the dignity of a born gentleman, yet stooping to be a tablebearer, an eavesdropper, a common butt in the taverns of London... Everything which another man would have hidden, everything the publication of which would have made another man hang himself, was a matter of exaltation to his weak and diseased mind.

***Thomas Babington Macaulay**, 1st Baron Macaulay (1800-1859), historian and MP. On poet James Boswell (1740-1795), Scottish biographer (particularly of Samuel Johnson)*

In the second century of the Christian Era, the empire of Rome comprehended the fairest part of the earth, and the most civilized portion of mankind. The frontiers of that extensive monarchy were guarded by ancient renown and disciplined valour. The gentle, but powerful influence of laws and manners had gradually cemented the union of the provinces. Their peaceful inhabitants enjoyed and abused the advantages of wealth and luxury. The image of a free constitution was preserved with decent reverence. The Roman senate appeared to possess the sovereign authority, and devolved on the emperors all the executive powers of government.

***Edward Gibbon** (1737-1794), historical writer, MP. Enrolled at Oxford aged 15. Opening paragraph of 'The History of the Decline and Fall of the Roman Empire'. Published 1776-1788 in six volumes*

'Is there any point to which you would wish to draw my attention?'
'To the curious incident of the dog in the night-time.'
'The dog did nothing in the night-time.'
'That was the curious incident,' remarked Sherlock Holmes.

***Sir Arthur Conan Doyle** (1859-1930), author, doctor, ship's surgeon.*
*Cricketer (ten first class matches), boxer, golfer. Spiritualist.*
*From 'The Adventures of Silver Blaze'*

I listened, motionless and still;
And, as I mounted up the hill,
The music in my heart I bore,
Long after it was heard no more.

***William Wordsworth** (1770-1850), Romantic poet.*
*Married four times. Poet Laureate*

He touched the horse with his heels and rode on. He rode with the sun coppering his face and the red wind blowing out of the west across the evening land and the small desert birds flew chattering among the dry bracken and horse and rider passed on and their long shadows passed in tandem like a single being. Passed and paled into the darkening land, the world to come.

***Cormac McCarthy** (born Charles McCarthy) (b 1933),*
*American novelist and playwright. From the end of his Western romance 'All the Pretty Horses'*

I have been in Sorrow's kitchen and licked out all the pots.
Then I have stood on the peaky mountain wrapped in rainbows, with a harp and sword in my hands.

***Zora Hurston** (1891-1960), American author, film maker and anthropologist*

And we beat on, in darkened boats against the current into the past.

***Francis Scott Fitzgerald** (1896-1940), American/Irish writer.*
*The last sentence of 'The Great Gatsby'*

## MUSIC

Music is the speech of angels.

***Thomas Carlyle** (1795-1881), historian, writer, philosopher, mathematician. Fluent German*

After playing Chopin, I fell as if I had been weeping over sins that I never committed and mourning over tragedies that were not my own.

***Oscar Wilde** (1854-1900), Irish playwright and poet*

A true music aficionado: A man who hears a beautiful woman singing in the bath and puts his ear to the keyhole.

*Quoted by Brian Kay (b1944), singer and choral conductor*

O Music! miraculous art! A blast of thy trumpet, and millions rush forward to die; a peal of thy organ, and uncounted nations sink down to pray.

***Benjamin Disraeli,** 1st Earl of Beaconsfield (1804-1881), politician, twice Prime Minister, novelist*

Music is the harmonious voice of creation; an echo of an invisible world; one note of the divine concord which the entire universe is destined one day to sound.

***Giuseppe Mazzini** (1805-1872), Italian politician, journalist. Activist for Italian unification*

Music has charms to soothe a savage breast, to soften rocks and bend the knotted oak.

***William Congreve** (1670-1729), poet, playwright and politician. From 'The Mourning Bride' (1697)*

Without music, life is a journey through a desert.

***Donald 'Pat' Conroy** (1945-2016), American novelist, film writer*

As long as we live, there is never enough singing. Next to the word of God, the noble art of music is the greatest treasure in the world-class.

***Martin Luther** (1483-1546), German theologist, priest, composer, Franciscan monk. Translated bible from Latin into German. Prolific writer of hymns*

Singing is so good a thing, I wish all men would learn to sing.

***William Byrd** (1540-1623), composer, organist.*
*Pupil of Thomas Tallis. Pioneer of the printing of music*

Music is an excellent thing. It reduces the beast in men.

***Joseph Stalin** (born Ioseb Besarionis dze Jughashvili) (1878-1953),*
*General Secretary of the Communist Party of the Soviet Union*
*1922-1952. As a choirboy had perfect pitch.*
*As a tenor, considered a professional singing career*

---

## LITERATURE

It was the best of times, it was the worst of times, it was the age of wisdom, it was the age of foolishness, it was the epoch of belief, it was the epoch of incredulity, it was the season of light, it was the season of darkness, it was the spring of hope, it was the winter of despair...

***Charles Dickens** (1812-1870), novelist and social critic.*
*Opening sentence from 'A Tale of Two Cities' –*
*the best selling novel of all time at 200 million*

In writing a novel, when in doubt, have two guys come through the door with guns.

***Raymond Chandler** (1888-1959), American/British novelist of*
*detective fiction. Gordon Highlander and Daily Express reporter*

I love being a writer. What I can't stand is the paperwork.

***Peter de Vries** (1910-1993), American novelist.*
*US Marine and reporter for The New Yorker*

*In 1986, the PHS (Printing House Square) column of The Times asked for readers' suggestions for the titles of notional biographies of the famous. These are some of the suggestions sent in:*

The Bungle Book. . . . . . . . . . . . . . . . . . . . . . . . .Ronald Reagan
Withering Heights. . . . . . . . . . . . . . . . . . . . . . . .Margaret Thatcher
The Merchant of Venus. . . . . . . . . . . . . . . . . . . .Hugh Heffner
Love, Labour's Lost. . . . . . . . . . . . . . . . . . . . . . .Tony Benn
Dr No . . . . . . . . . . . . . . . . . . . . . . . . . . . . . . . .Ian Paisley
Redhead Sails in the Fun-Set . . . . . . . . . . . . . . . .Sarah Ferguson
Redhead Revisited. . . . . . . . . . . . . . . . . . . . . . . .John Timpson
Maidenhead Revisited . . . . . . . . . . . . . . . . . . . . .Roman Polanski
Decline and Fall of the British Umpire. . . . . . . . .John McEnroe
Who Bares Wins . . . . . . . . . . . . . . . . . . . . . . . . .Paul Raymond
A Cue From the Bridge . . . . . . . . . . . . . . . . . . . .Steve Davis
Peas in our Time . . . . . . . . . . . . . . . . . . . . . . . .Robert Carrier
Tristan's Handy . . . . . . . . . . . . . . . . . . . . . . . . .Isolde
Gone for a Burton. . . . . . . . . . . . . . . . . . . . . . . .Elizabeth Taylor

The first thing a writer has to do is to find another source of income.

***Ellen Gilchrist** (b 1935), American short story writer.*
*Four marriages and divorces*

Libraries are the wardrobes of literature.

Me, poor man, my library
Was dukedom large enough.

***William Shakespeare**, 'The Tempest'*

A library is a room where murders take place.

***John Morton*** *(John Cameron Andrieu Bingham Michael Morton) (1893-1979), writer noted for Beachcomber column in Daily Express*

How still and peaceful is a Library! It seems quiet as the grave, tranquil as heaven, a cool collection of the thoughts of the men of all times. And yet, approach and open the pages, and you find them full of dissension and disputes, alive with abuse and detraction – a huge, many-volumed satire upon man, written by himself... What a broad thing is a library – all shades of opinion reflected on its catholic bosom, as the sunbeams and shadows of a summer's day upon the ample mirror of a lake.

***George Gilfillan*** *(1813-1878), Scottish author and poet*

The covers of this book are too far apart.

***Ambrose Bierce*** *(1842-1914), American author, poet. One of 13 children all named starting with 'A'. Officer in Union army*

The easiest reading is damned hard writing.

***Thomas Hood*** *(1799-1845), poet, author and humourist*

I hate having new books forced upon me, but how I love cramming them down the throats of other people!

*Anon*

As the hours crept by, the afternoon sunlight bleached all the books on the shelves to pale, gilded versions of themselves and warmed the paper and ink inside the covers so that the smell of unread words hung in the air.

*Margaret Stiefvater (b 1981), American novelist –*
*30 novels by age twenty. Stunt car driver*

*Georges Simenon (1903-1989) was the Belgian creator of the French detective Maigret. By the time he died, he had written nearly 200 novels, more than 150 novellas, several memoirs and countless short stories. The books were written fast, without outline and needed minimal correction. Simenon demanded silence, writing one Maigret story a week. When Alfred Hitchcock telephoned one day, he was told* 'Sorry, he's just started a novel'. 'That's all right, I'll wait,' *came the reply.*

The original motto of Penguin books was 'Good books, cheap' and in those days they cost sixpence a volume. In the early days they were colour-coded:

ORANGE . . . . . . . . . . . . for fiction
GREEN. . . . . . . . . . . . . . for crime
LIGHT BLUE . . . . . . . . . for non-fiction
DARK BLUE. . . . . . . . . . for biography
CERISE. . . . . . . . . . . . . . for travel
RED . . . . . . . . . . . . . . . . for theatre
YELLOW . . . . . . . . . . . . for miscellany

The Penguin paperback was the original in 1935, with Pelican following in 1937 and Puffin paperbacks, specifically for children, coming out in 1956.

*The British Library:*

- It receives a copy of every publication produced in the UK and Ireland.
- The collection includes 150 million items, in most known languages, dating from 300 BC to the present day.
- Three million new items are incorporated every year.
- It holds manuscripts, maps, newspapers, magazines, prints and drawings, music scores, and patents.
- The Sound Archive keeps sound recordings from nineteenth-century cylinders to the latest CD, DVD and minidisc recordings.
- The collection includes 310,000 manuscript volumes, from Jane Austen to the Beatles.
- It houses 8 million stamps and other philatelic items, 49.5 million patents, 4 million maps and over 260,000 journal titles.
- The shelf space grows by 12 kilometres every year.
- Its key possessions include the *Magna Carta*, the *Lindisfarne Gospels*, the first dated printed book, *The Diamond Sutra*, Leonardo da Vinci's *Notebook*, the first edition of *The Times* from 18 March 1788 and the recording of Nelson Mandela's trial speech.
- The building at St Pancras was the largest public building constructed in the UK in the twentieth century.

*The Harry Potter phenomenon:*

Book five of the Harry Potter series holds the record for the largest print run in history. Thirteen million hardback copies of *Harry Potter and the Order of the Phoenix* were printed, 875,000 advance orders taken on Amazon.com alone. *Harry Potter and the Goblet of Fire* (book four) holds the record for the most advance orders: 5.3 million copies (about 40 times as many as the average bestseller).

---

I've always imagined that Paradise will be a kind of library.

***Jorge Borges Acevedo** (1899-1986), Argentinian writer, poet. Bilingual Spanish and English. Fluent in German and Italian*

There is no friend so loyal as a good book.

***Ernest Hemingway** (1899-1961), American novelist, journalist, sportsman*

A good book on your shelf is a friend that turns its back to you and remains a friend.

***Laurence J Peter** (1919-1990), Canadian educator. Originator of The Peter Principle, 'Every employee rises to the level of his incompetence'*

Choose an author as you would a friend.

***Wentworth Dillon, 4th Earl of Roscommon** (1633-1685), Irish peer and poet*

We were put to Dickens as children but it never quite took. That unremitting humanity soon had me cheesed off.

***Alan Bennett** (b 1934), playwright, screenwriter, actor, author. Medievalist at Oxford*

The smallest bookstore still contains more ideas of worth than have been presented in the entire history of television.

***Andrew Ross** (b 1956), American sociologist. Nobel Prize for Literature, 1996*

No furniture is so charming as books, even if you never open them or read a single word.

***Rev Sidney Smith** (1739-1827), Canon of St Paul's Cathedral. Aulae Praeceptor at Winchester College. Scholarship to New College, Oxford. Double first*

What we become depends on what we read after all the professors have finished with us. The greatest university of all is a collection of books.

***Thomas Carlyle** (1795-1881), historian, philosopher, mathematician*

*Descriptions of Hay-on-Wye, the venue of the famous literary festival, vary from the idyllic* 'Hay-on-Wye is the Woodstock of the mind' ***(Bill Clinton)*** *to* 'Is it some sort of sandwich?' ***(Arthur Miller).***

In America only the successful writer is important, in France all writers are important, in England no writer is important, in Australia you have to explain what a writer is.

***Geoffrey Cotterell** (1919-2010), novelist*

*Many women writers, particularly in the 18th and 19th centuries, hid behind a pseudonym. These are some of them:*

Mary Ann Evans . . . . . . . . . . . . writing as George Eliot
Amantine Aurore Dupin . . . . . . writing as George Sand
Mary Bright . . . . . . . . . . . . . . . writing as George Egerton
Julia Constance Fleming . . . . . . writing as George Fleming
Emily Bronte. . . . . . . . . . . . . . . writing as Ellis Bell
Charlotte Bronte. . . . . . . . . . . . writing as Currer Bell
Joanne Rowling. . . . . . . . . . . . . writing as Robert Galbraith
Violet Page . . . . . . . . . . . . . . . . writing as Vernon Lee

So please, oh please, we beg, we pray,
Throw your TV set away
And in its place you can install
A lovely bookcase on the wall

***Roald Dahl** (1916-1990), British children's writer of Norwegian parentage. Pilot, diplomat, intelligence officer.*

*There are only three films which have won Oscars for Best Picture, Best Director, Best Actor, Best Actress and Best Screenplay:* It Happened One Night *(1934)*; One Flew Over the Cuckoo's Nest *(1975)*; and The Silence of the Lambs *(1991)*.

Mickey Mouse receives 66,000 fan letters a month.

Cinema is the most beautiful fraud in the world.

***Jean-Luc Godard** (b 1930), French/Swiss film director, screenwriter and critic. Pioneer of New Wave Film Movement. Marxist*

Although I can accept talking scarecrows, lions and great wizards of emerald cities, I find it hard to believe there is no paperwork involved when your house lands on a witch.

***Dave James**, script writer and radio presenter*

If you suck on a tit, the movie gets an R rating. If you hack it off with an axe it will be PG.

***Jack Nicholson**, (born John Joseph Nicholson) (b 1937), American actor and filmmaker. 12 Academy Award Nominations, three Awards. 66 films*

The only thing worse than watching a bad movie is being in one.

***Elvis Presley** (1935-1977), American singer and actor*

It is probable that the movie fad will die out in the next few years.

*The Independent, US newspaper, 1910*

It's like being assaulted by a gang of singing cherubs wielding sticks of candyfloss.

***Cosmo Landesman,*** *American journalist and editor.*
*About the film 'Love Actually', 2003*

*Common to all movies:*

- Mothers always cook breakfast for their families, who then don't have time to finish them.
- If someone is having a nightmare, they will wake up by sitting bolt upright in bed.
- All bombs constructed by madmen have a large red display of the time left before they explode.
- Deciphering the password for a computer system will only take a few attempts.
- Even if a person is in their mid-twenties, as long as they are stunningly attractive it is possible for them to be a world expert on genetics/nuclear fission/biological warfare and astrophysics.
- No matter how virginal and sheltered the heroine, at the moment of crisis it turns out that all along she has been an expert at kick boxing.
- There is always a space to park a car.
- Suitcases, trunks and portmanteau are always so light they must be empty.

*Jobs in the film industry you have never understood:*

Foley Artist . . . Person creating sound effects
Gaffer . . . . . . . Chief lighting technician
Best Boy . . . . . Assistant to the Gaffer. Female assistants are also Best Boys
Grip . . . . . . . . Crew member responsible for building and maintaining camera equipment and supports.
Key Grip . . . . . The chief grip working with the Gaffer
Dolly Grip. . . . Crew member moving the Dolly, a small camera-carrying truck on rails
Greensman . . . Crew member who maintains any vegetation on set
Swing Gang. . . Group that constructs or demolishes a set
Leadman . . . . . In charge of the Swing Gang

---

*Famous one liners:*

'Go ahead, make my day.'
*Clint Eastwood, Magnum Force (1973); Sudden Impact (1983)*

'Frankly, my dear, I don't give a damn.'
*Clark Gable, Gone With the Wind (1939)*

'Here's looking at you, kid.'
*Humphrey Bogart, Casablanca (1942)*

'Show me the money!'
*Cuba Gooding Jr, Jerry Maguire (1996)*

'We want the finest wines available to humanity,
we want them here and we want them now.'
*Richard E Grant, Withnail and I (1987)*

'You were only supposed to blow the bloody doors off!'
*Michael Caine, The Italian Job (1969)*

'You talkin' to me?'
*Robert De Niro, Taxi Driver (1976)*

'I'll have what she's having.'
*Estelle Reiner, When Harry met Sally (1989)*

'I do wish we could chat longer. But I'm having an old friend for dinner.'
*Anthony Hopkins, The Silence of the Lambs (1991)*

'Who are these men?'
*Paul Newman, Butch Cassidy and the Sundance Kid (1969)*

---

*Extracts from 'Seeing in the Dark. A Compendium of Cinemagoing', 1990:*

In the 1930s you learnt how to behave as a human being from movies. You learnt how to smoke, how to hold a cigarette. I wanted to become a reporter because I lusted after a belted trenchcoat like the one Joel McCrea wore in Hitchcock's Foreign Correspondence. Girls kissed with their eyes closed and raising themselves up on tiptoe, because that was the cute shot in American movies. We believed in Hollywood. Cinemas themselves were special. Nobody had central heating, so it was warm. It was dark: 'six penn'orth of dark' was what people were after. The cinema was our motel. And it was opulent in the way nothing else in your life was. They were called 'picture palaces' for a very good reason. At the Empire, Leicester Square, the toilets were truly lavish: 'I dreamt I dwelt in marble halls' had real meaning. Before the cinema opened the men on the staff were given cigars to puff, so that when you came into the foyer it had that smell of luxury.

***Denis Norden** (1922-2018), comedy writer, TV and radio presenter*

But Dumbo was different. We carried sticky ice cream cones into the large dark room. We each had to sit in our own chair. I had crawled into mine and was turning round peering into the dark where many people sat eating popcorn and candy. My parents were pointing up to a beam of light, and saying, 'Dumbo'. I stared at a huge rectangle of light, it was pinkish floating flickering and suddenly I saw... a pig! 'Piglet!' I yelled. Piglet was up there! From the book I held on my lap! Piglet who I improved with blue and green crayons was here, huge, powerful, incandescent, unreachable and in motion! I sank into an exquisite passivity staring ahead as dazzling colours flushed and flew, metamorphosing into duck and elephant cat dog house. My parents were happy and proud that I was finally seeing what they saw.

***Carolee Schneemann** (1939-2019), American experimental artist*

The sign over the box office of the Majestic cinema, Rathby, Leicestershire in the mid 1950s read: 'It's warmer inside'. In summer the word 'warmer' was covered by a wooden panel, hung on the nails, which read 'cooler'. Beneath this, another sign reassured us that 'This cinema is treated with DDT'.

***Chris Garratt**, script writer and experimental film maker*

In 1954 I was eight and every Saturday morning I would set off to the movies with my first boyfriend, ten-year-old Skippy. For several hours we would be transported via the newsreel to the exotic East, where American soldiers were valiantly fighting the red, or was it yellow peril, and then to the Wild West, where Hoot Gibson or Eddy Dean would be showing cattle rustlers or unfriendly Indians 'what America stood for'. We would spend the afternoon re-enacting in the parking lot behind the apartment what we had just seen in the morning on the screen. It was then that I began to discover the fate that awaited me as a female. Whilst I saw myself as the hero's faithful sidekick, got up as I was in cowboy gloves with real leather fringes, two guns in holsters buckled on and tied around the leg for the last draw, ten gallon hat and waistcoat, Skippy insisted that I be the daughter of the murdered rancher whose cattle were being rustled. Gradually it began to dawn on me that while in the celluloid world all things were possible, in the other world it was quite a different story.

*Marlene Winfield, American film actress*

---

*The first Star Wars was made in 1976. It was turned down by all the major studios until accepted by 20th Century Fox. Its minimal budget of $11m meant that much of the set was created from old aircraft and breakers yards. It grossed $765m. The current film The Last Jedi cost $200m and made $745m in its first two weeks.*

*Mike Berlin (a lecturer at V&A in 2020) was once part of a team that hoped to make a film from Rose Tremain's book Restoration. In the pitch to a studio they outlined the plot.* 'A physician in medieval London, the Great Plague, followed by the Great Fire'. 'No. No,' *cried the studio.* 'Nobody is going to believe that a plague was followed by a fire.' *The film was so bad that Tremain asked for her name to be taken off the credits.*

*Film critics:*

*On the 1959 remake of Ben-Hur:* "Loved Ben, Hated Hur"
*Of the 1955 film I am a Camera:* "Me no Leica"

---

Hollywood is a place where they'll pay you a thousand dollars for a kiss, and fifty cents for your soul.

***Marilyn Monroe** (born Norma Mortenson) (1926-1962),*
*American actress, model and singer. Thirty films.*

# 5 | Poetry and Lyrics

She was poor but she was honest
Victim of a rich man's game.
First he loved her, then he left her,
And she lost her maiden name...

It's the same the whole world over,
It's the poor wot gets the blame,
It's the rich wot gets the gravy.
Ain't it all a bleedin' shame?

*Music hall song of World War One.*
*Later a British rugby song*

THE EAGLE

He clasps the crag with crooked hands;
Close to the sun in lonely lands,
Ring'd with the azure world, he stands.
The wrinkled sea beneath him crawls;
He watches from his mountain walls,
And like a thunderbolt he falls.

***Lord Alfred Tennyson** (1809-1892), poet.*
*Poet Laureate*

Edgar Allan Poe
Was fond of roe
He liked to chew some
While writing something gruesome.

George the Third
Should never have occurred
One can only wonder
At so grotesque a blunder.

God in his wisdom made the fly
And then forgot to tell us why.

*__Ogden Nash__ (1902-1971),*
*American poet of light verse*

THE TRUE BORN ENGLISHMAN

Thus from a mixture of all kinds began,
That het'rogeneous thing, an Englishman:
In eager rapes, and furious lust begot,
Betwixt a painted Britain and a Scot.
Whose gend'ring off-spring quickly learn'd to bow,
And yoke their heifers to the Roman plough:

From whence a mongrel half-bred race there came,
With neither name, nor nation, speech nor fame.
In whose hot veins new mixtures quickly ran,
Infus'd betwixt a Saxon and a Dane.
While their rank daughters, to their parents just,
Receiv'd all nations with promiscuous lust.
This nauseous brood directly did contain
The well-extracted blood of Englishmen.

A true-born Englishman's a contradiction,
In speech an irony, in fact a fiction.

Since scarce one family is left alive,
Which does not from some foreigner derive.

***Daniel Defoe** (born Daniel Foe) (1660-1731), journalist, novelist and spy. 545 published books and pamphlets*

Where are the kings, and where the rest
Of those who once the world possessed?

They're gone with all their pomp and show,
They're gone the way that thou shalt go.

O thou who choosest for thy share
The world, and what the world calls fair,

Take all that it can give or lend,
But know that death is at the end.

***Henry Wadsworth Longfellow** (1807-1882), American poet. Fluent in Latin and translated Dante's Divine Comedy. One of the Fireside Poets of New England*

***Gerald Durrell** (1925-1995) was well known as a naturalist, animal collector, television presenter and zookeeper. He was also a proficient exponent of verse and poetry. Here are three examples taken from Douglas Botting's biography 'Gerald Durrell' published in 1999:*

Up in the snow covered Andes,
There's only one beast you will see,
Who is clever enough to learn all the stuff
That one needs to obtain a degree.

The Spectacled Bear is a wonder,
The Spectacled Bear is no fool,
The Spectacled Bear, with a wisdom that's rare,
Paid attention when he went to school.

The Spectacled Bear learnt Spanish,
The Spectacled Bear learnt to draw,
The Spectacled Bear with time and with care,
Could multiply twenty by four.

But one day someone gave him a parrot,
(A bird that was badly behaved),
But one thing it did well, and that was to spell,
So the Spectacled Bear was saved.

With this bird as his constant companion
He writes letters to friends now with glee,
And always, you'll find they are carefully signed:
'Spectickled Bere, B.Sc.'

So if ever your teacher should ask you
To spell words like 'Zephyr' or 'Claret',
The thing I'd suggest that would be the best
Is to go out and purchase a parrot.

Of all the places I have bin ta
I have seen some luscious dames.
Blonde, beguiling redheads yummy,
Chocolate skins with jewels in tummy,
Skins like sexy yellow silk,
Skins like roses, skins like milk,
Bosom, buttock, legs a-twinkle,
Girls who have not got a wrinkle.
Girls beguiling, smiles so winning,
Girls who like a bit of sinning.
But in all the places that I've bin ta
None compare with Araminta.

I have seen a thousand sunsets and sunrises,
On land where it floods forest and mountains with honey coloured light:
I have seen a thousand moons...
I have felt winds as tender and warm as a lover's breath;
Winds that carried the moist rich smell of a forest floor,
The smell of a million flowers...
I have known silence:
The hot, drugged silence when everything is stilled by the eye of the sun;
The silence when great music ends...

*Ibid*

# 6 | Countryside and Nature

*British moths:*

Common Swift
The Shark
Reed Leopard
Peach Blossom
Wood Tiger
The Stranger
Bearded Chestnut
The Basker
The Non Conformist
The Suspected
The Confused
The Uncertain
The Delicate
Dog's Tooth
Isabelline Tiger
Waved Tabby

---

*Wildlife named after famous people:*

Mastophora dizzydeani . . . . . . . . . . . . a spider
*(named for baseball player 'Dizzy' Dean)*

Campsicnemus charlie-chaplini . . . . . . a fly

Baeturia laureli & Baeturia hardyi. . . . cicadas

Bufonaria borisbeckeri . . . . . . . . . . . . a sea snail

My father told me all about the birds and the bees; the liar.
I went steady with a woodpecker until I was 21.

*__Bob Hope__ (born Leslie Townes Hope) (1903-2003), American comedian, actor, singer. 54 films, author of 14 books. Father, stonemason from Somerset*

We think caged birds sing when in fact, they cry.

*__John Webster__ (1580-1632), Jacobean dramatist, 'Duchess of Malfi', and barrister*

God loved birds and gave them trees,
Man loved birds and gave them cages.

*__Jean-Jacques Duval__ (b 1980), French artist of stained glass*

In Flanders fields the poppies blow
Between the crosses, row on row,
That mark our place; and in the sky
The larks, still bravely singing, fly
Scarce heard amid the guns below.

*__John McCrae__ (1872-1918), Canadian poet, doctor, author, artist. From 'In Flanders Fields' 1915*

He who plants a tree, plants hope.

*__Lucy Larcom__ (1824-1893), American poet*

Bugs are not going to inherit the Earth. They own it now.
We might as well make peace with the Landlord.

*__Thomas Eisner__ (1929-2011), German/American entomologist. 400 published scientific papers. Honorary degrees from five European universities*

If Eve had had a spade in Paradise, we should not have had all that sad business of the apple.

*__Elisabeth von Arnim__ (1866-1941), Australian novelist.*
*By marriage Countess von Arnim-Schlagenthin.*
*Wrote under name of Alice Cholmondeley*

*Nature collectives:*

A cete of badgers
A drift of bees
A peep of chickens
A piteousness of doves
A business of ferrets
A charm of finches
A kindle of kittens
A tiding of magpies
A richesse of martins
A labour of moles
A wedge of swans
A herd of wrens
A skulk of foxes

*Book of St Albans, 1486*

Il me faut surtout avoir des fleurs, toujours, toujours.
[More than anything I must have flowers, always, always.]

***Oscar-Claude Monet** (1840-1926), French founder of Impressionist painting. Seven years with African Light Cavalry*

Sir, 'Tantony' is a new name to me for the small one of a litter of pigs or dogs. Some years ago I made the following collection of names all in use in various parts of the country:

Nisgil (Midlands), Nisledrige and Nestletripe (Devon), Darling, Daniel, Dolly and Harry (Hants), Underling, Rickling, Reckling, Little David (Kent), Dillin, Dilling (Stratford-on-Avon), Cad, Gramper, Nestletribe, Nestledrag, Nestlebird, Dab-Chick, Wastrill, Weed, Dandlin, Anthony, Runt, Parson's Pig (the least valuable to be devoted to tithe purposes), Nest Squab, Putman, Ratling, Dorneedy (Scottish), The Titman (Vermont), Nestledraft, Pigot, Rutland, Luchan, Piggy-Widden.

*The Times. June 1923*

I dug
I levelled
I weeded
I seeded
I planted
I waited
I weeded
I pleaded
I mulched
I gulched
I watered
I waited
I fumbled
I grumbled
I poked
I hoped
So GROW, dammit

***Diana Anthony**, gardening writer*

*Animal walking styles:*

- A donkey can see all four of its feet at once.
- Newfoundland dogs are strong swimmers and have webbed feet.
- Polar bears are the only mammals with hair on the soles of their feet.
- Butterflies taste with their back feet.
- Elephants walk on tiptoe as the back part of their feet is only fat.
- Cats step with both left legs, then both right legs. Only camels and giraffes do this as well.

---

*Patrick Leigh Fermor takes stock during a Carpathian upland walk:*

I feared I might have got rusty, but all was well and my kit seemed in as good repair as the first day in Holland. The ammunition boots from Millets in the Strand, crunching along on their only slightly blunted hobnails, were still good for unlimited miles. The old breeches were soft with much wear and cleaning, and every stitch was intact; only the grey puttees had suffered minor damage, but nothing showed when I had snipped off the ragged edges where snow and rain had frayed them. A grey shirt with the sleeves rolled up completed this marching gear.

I blessed my stars that my first rucksack, with its complex framework and straps, heavy water-proof sleeping-bag and White Knight superfluity of gear had been stolen in Munich; the one my Baltic Russian friends had bestowed was smaller but held all I needed; to wit: a pair of dark flannel bags and another light canvas pair; a thick, decent-looking tweed jacket; several shirts; two ties, gym-shoes, lots of socks and jerseys, pyjamas, the length of coloured braid Angela had given me; a dozen new handkerchiefs and a sponge-bag, a compass, a jack-knife, two candles, matches, a pipe – falling into disuse – tobacco, cigarettes and – a new accomplishment – papers for rolling them, and a flask-filled in turn, as the countries changed, with whisky, Bols, schnapps, barack, tzuica, slivovitz, arak and tziporo. In one of the side pockets there was a five-shilling Ingersoll watch that kept perfect time when I remembered to take it out and wind it up.

The only awkward item was the soldier's greatcoat; I hadn't worn it for months, but felt reluctant to get rid of it. I still had the Hungarian walking-stick, intricately carved as a mediaeval crosier, the second replacement for the original ninepenny ashplant from the tobacconist's off Sloane Square. Apart from sketch-book, pencils and disintegrating maps, there was my notebook-journal and my passport. (Dog-eared and faded, these sole survivors are both within reach at this moment.) There was Hungarian and Rumanian Self-Taught (little progress in the one, hesitant first steps in the other); I was re-reading Antic Hay; and there was Schlegel & Tieck's Hamlet, Prinz von Danemark, bought in Cologne.

It would have been hard to set off much later than the cock crew that morning as the bird itself was flapping its wings on a barrel ten yards away, so I shoshed some water on my face and set off. It was going to be a sizzling day.

***Sir Patrick Leigh Fermor (known as Paddy) (1915-2011), author, soldier, scholar and polyglot.*** *From 'Between the Woods and the Water' 1933*

My grandmother started walking five miles a day when she was 60. She is 97 today and we don't know where the hell she is.

***Ellen Degeneres*** *(b 1958), American gay comedian, actress, writer and activist. 30 Emmy awards. 15th highest paid entertainer in the world.*

Walk a day, live a week.

*French proverb*

One day in the country is worth a week in town.

***Christina Rossetti*** *(1830-1894), Romantic poet, sister of Dante Gabriel Rossetti*

That gracious thing, made up of tears and light.

***Samuel Coleridge** (1772-1834), poet philosopher, theologian. German translator*

That smiling daughter of the storm.

***Charles Colton** (1777-1832), eccentric cleric and writer. Wine collector, gambler*

---

I had a rose named after me and I was very flattered. But I was not pleased to read the description in the catalogue: 'No good in a bed, but fine against a wall'.

***Eleanor Roosevelt** (1884-1962), American First Lady and activist*

Dull was twinned with Boring years ago; now Bland has got in on the act. The union of dreary towns began in 2012, when a resident of Dull, in Perthshire, visited Boring during a trip to Oregon. The towns saw a chance to boost tourism; and last month Bland, in Australia, was formally welcomed into 'The League of Extraordinary Communities'.

*The Week, 2017*

Thou wast not born for death, Immortal Bird!
No hungry generations tread thee down;
The voice I hear this passing night was heard
In ancient days by emperor and clown.

***John Keats** (1795-1828), Romantic poet. Qualified surgeon. From 'Ode to a Nightingale', 1819.*

'Down here in Dorset we have Ryme Intrinseca as distinct from Ryme Extrinseca. Sadly, Extrinseca is now redundant.'

The last word, though, should probably go to James Cellan Jones of Wells. 'My aunt lived most of her life in Wales, but retired to live in Kent. Travelling home by bus, she passed through Thanington Without. One of two American ladies sitting behind her asked, 'Thanington Without? Without what?'

'Sanitation, I guess,' said her friend.

*Purple Emperor butterflies:*

Transparent forms too fine for mortal sight
Their fluid bodies half dissolved in light,
Loose to the wind their airy garments flew,
Thin glittering textures of the filmy dew,
Dipt in the richest tincture of the skies,
Where light disports in ever-mingling dyes;
While ev'ry beam new transient colours flings,
Colours that change whene'er they wave their wings.

***Alexander Pope*** *(1688-1744), poet, satirist.*
*Translated Homer's The Iliad and Odyssey in five volumes*

Green was the silence, wet was the light, the month of June trembled like a butterfly.

***Pablo Neruda** (born Ricardo Basoalta) (1904-1973), Chilean poet, diplomat. Nobel Prize for Literature. Lewin Peace Prize*

The love of gardening is a seed once sown that never dies.

***Gertrude Jekyll** (1843-1932), horticulturist, garden designer, photographer, artist, writer. Created over 400 gardens*

He who plants a garden, plants happiness.

*Anon*

A garden is a delight to the eye and a solace for the soul.

***Saadi Shiraz** (1210-1292), Persian poet, traveller. Sunni muslim*

To plant a garden is to believe in tomorrow.

***Audrey Hepburn,** born Audrey Ruston (1929-1993), daughter of Baroness Ella von Heemstra and Joseph Hepburn-Ruston. Scholarship to Ballet Rambert. Global Ambassador for UNICEF. Four Academy nominations. Three BAFTA awards.*

# 7 | Prayers, religion and morality

An eye for an eye will only make the whole world blind.

***Mohandas 'Mahatma' Gandhi*** *(1869-1948),*
Indian lawyer, nationalist and political activist

Yesterday is history, tomorrow is a mystery, today is a gift of God, which is why we call it the present.

***William Keane*** *(Bill) (1922-2011), American cartoonist*

Don't hurry, don't worry. You're only here for a short visit. So be sure to stop and smell the flowers.

***Walter Hagen*** *(1892-1969), American professional golfer.*
*Winner of US and UK Open and PGA five times.*
*First golfer to win $1 million*

HERE, AT WHATEVER HOUR YOU COME,
YOU WILL FIND LIGHT, HELP AND HUMAN KINDNESS

***Dr Albert Schweitzer*** *(1875-1965), German theologian,*
*philosopher and physician. Inscription on the lamp*
*outside his hospital at Lambaréné, Gabon*

Life is pleasant. Death is peaceful. It's the transition that's troublesome.

***Isaac Asimov** (1920-1992), American/Russian biochemist and science fiction writer*

The Jews and Arabs should settle their dispute in the true spirit of Christian charity.

***Alexander Wiley** (1884-1967), American politician. Four terms as United States Senator*

I'm so holy that when I touch wine, it turns to water.

***Sir Sultan Shah, Aga Khan III** (1877-1957), Imam of Shia Muslims. Eton and Cambridge. Sixteen winners of Classic horse races*

In heaven, all the interesting people are missing.

***Friedrich Nietzsche** (1844-1900), German philosopher, critic, poet, classical philologist and composer*

In heaven an angel is nobody particular.

***George Bernard Shaw** (1856-1950), Irish playwright (60 plays) and critic. Promoted eugenics and reform of the alphabet. Opposed vaccination and religions*

God has given us music so that above all it can lead us upwards. Music unites all qualities: it can exalt us, divert us, cheer us up, or breaks the hardest of hearts with the softest of its melancholy tones.

*Ibid*

Life doesn't imitate art, it imitates bad television.

***Heywood 'Woody' Allen*** *(born Allan Konisberg) (b 1935), American actor, writer, film maker and comedian*

Let your heart be your compass, your mind your map and your soul your guide, then you will never get lost.

***Ritu Ghatourey****, Indian writer*

*The Rev Dr Edward Everett Hale, the popular American Unitarian minister who became Chaplain to the United States Senate, was asked if he started each day by praying for the senators. He responded,* 'No, I look at them and I pray for the country'.

***Rev Dr Edward Everett Hale*** *(1822-1922). Enrolled at Harvard aged thirteen*

*A prayer for the middle-aged:*

Lord, Thou knowest better than I know myself that I am growing older and will some day be old. Keep me from the fatal habit of thinking I must say something on every subject and on every occasion. Release me from craving to straighten out everybody's affairs. Make me thoughtful but not moody, helpful but not bossy. With my vast store of wisdom, it seems a pity not to use it all, but Thou knowest, Lord, that I want a few friends at the end.

Keep my mind from the recital of endless details; give me wings to get to the point. Seal my lips on my aches and pains. They are increasing, and the love of rehearsing them is becoming sweeter as the years go by. I dare not ask for grace enough to enjoy the tales of others' pains, but help me to endure them with patience.

I dare not ask for improved memory, but for a growing humility, and a lessening cocksureness when my memory seems to clash with the memories of others. Teach me the glorious lesson that occasionally I may be mistaken.

Keep me reasonably sweet; I do not want to be a Saint – some of them are so hard to live with – but a sour person is one of the crowning works of the devil. Give me the ability to see good things in unexpected places, and talents in unexpected people. And give me, O Lord, the grace to tell them so.

*Seventeenth century nuns' prayer. Quoted on BBC 'Woman's Hour', October 1976*

Buy old masters. They fetch a much better price than old mistresses.

***William Aitken, 1st Baron Beaverbrook** (1879-1964), Canadian/British newspaper publisher. Wartime minister*

# 8 Miscellaneous

Everything can be filed under miscellaneous.

***George Bernard Shaw** (1856-1950), Irish playwright, critic, political activist. 60 plays. Nobel Prize for Literature, 1925*

'I must telephone the Vatican' *was **Noel Coward's** way, at a social gathering, of saying he needed to visit the loo.*

He looks like an unmade bed.

***'Bobby' Salisbury, Robert Gascoyne-Cecil, 5th Marquess of Salisbury** (1893-1972), about Michael Ramsey (1904-1989), Archbishop of Canterbury.*

Most Provosts leave for Heaven but I am going to Bournemouth.

***Lord Hugh Cecil, Baron Quickswood** (1869-1956), on saying goodbye to Fellows of Eton. Nicknamed Linky by his brothers who saw a resemblance to the Missing Link between ape and man.*

***Jonathan Gascoyne-Cecil** (1939-2011), actor and son of Lord David Cecil, was asked as a boy what he wanted to be when he grew up:* 'A neurotic, like Father'.

*After watching the Olympic Horse Trials at Badminton,* ***Kenneth Rose*** *wrote:* 'Vast crowds of people, most upper-middle-class, the women with voices one supposes breeds Communism'.

You mentioned your name as if I should recognise it, but beyond the obvious fact that you are a bachelor, a solicitor, a Freemason, and an asthmatic, I know nothing whatever about you.

*From 'The Adventure of the Norwood Builder' by* ***Sir Arthur Conan Doyle.*** *Published in 'Strand Magazine', 1903*

My ignorance of science is such that if anyone mentioned copper nitrate I should think he was talking about a policeman's overtime.

***Donald Coggan, Baron Coggan*** *(1909-2000), 101st Archbishop of Canterbury. Double first at Cambridge. Fluent in Hebrew, Aramaic, Syriac, Latin and Greek*

***The Rt Revd Percy Herbert*** *(1885-1968), Bishop of Norwich 1942-1959, was an enthusiastic shot. Arriving at a shoot, he discovered he had brought the case containing his crozier. He was philosophical about it* – 'Not as bad as taking my shotgun to a confirmation'.

Middle class girls get degrees. The working class get jobs. The underclass get a baby as soon as they can.

***Tony Parsons*** *(b 1953), journalist and novelist*

Sir, Giles Coren's piece ('Get off the couch Fido', July 20) reminds me of the patient suffering an identity crisis who consults his doctor. 'Doctor, I think I'm turning into a dog.' His doctor replies: 'I'd better examine you. Go and lie down on the couch'. The man replies: 'I'm not allowed on the couch'.

The requirements of a successful governor of the Bank of England are the tact and skill of an ambassador and the guile of a Romanian horse thief.

***Harold Lever, Baron Lever of Manchester** (1914-1995), barrister and Labour minister*

The *Daily Mirror* is read by the people who think they run the country. *The Guardian* is read by people who think they *ought* to run the country. *The Times* is read by the people who actually *do* run the country. The *Daily Mail* is read by the *wives* of the people who run the country. The *Morning Star* is read by people who think the country ought to be run by *another* country. *The Daily Telegraph* is read by the people who think it is. And *The Sun* readers don't care who runs the country – as long as she's got big tits.

*PM Jim Hacker in 'Yes, Prime Minister'. Television satirical sitcom by Antony Jay and Jonathon Lynn. Ran for 38 episodes from 1980*

Sir, Regarding Rose Wild's reference to Ian Carman's remark about shoppers having £10 billion worth of clothes that they don't wear in their wardrobes, in our village we regularly have signs advertising a 'Giant Rug Sale'. I can assure you that the rugs are not giant. Similarly, I recently bought some drops for a sore eye. The packaging reads: 'Infected Eye Drops'.

*The Times, January, 2018*

*Cricket:*

The English are not a very spiritual people, so they invented cricket to give them some idea of eternity.

***George Bernard Shaw** (1856-1950), Irish playwright, critic and political activist. 56 plays – full length and short*

Cricket is basically baseball on valium.

***Robin Williams** (1951-2014, suicide), American actor and comedian. Four Academy awards. Scholarship to Juilliard*

Having watched a match at Lord's for several hours, Michael Davies asked: 'Are you enjoying it?' Groucho Marx replied: 'It's great. When does it start?'

***Daniel Lightman**, QC, Lincoln's Inn, London WC2*

Rice bowls and Paddy fields. I've been waiting all afternoon to say that.

***John Arlott** (1914-1991), journalist and cricket commentator. 12 published books. Mental hospital nurse, policeman, boxer, Russian speaker.*

Sir, Foakes, Stokes and Woakes (letter, Oct 29) may indeed make a rhyming team sheet, but it is difficult to see them having the same impact as 'Lillee caught Willey bowled Dilley' during the second innings of the first Test between Australia and England in Brisbane in 1979-80.

*The Times*

Sir, Further to the previous letters on the subject of notable cricketing scorecard entries (Oct 29, 30 & 31), the dismissal of the England captain, George Mann, by the South African spin bowler 'Tufty' Mann during England's 1948-49 tour to South Africa prompted the broadcaster John Arlott to describe it as 'a case of Mann's inhumanity to Mann'.

*The Times*

*Football:*

Football is all very well. A good game for rough girls, but not for delicate boys.

***Oscar Wilde** (1854-1900), flamboyant Irish poet and playwright*

Without football, it's impossible to live.

***Mauricio Pochettino** (b 1972), Argentinian manager of Tottenham Hotspur*

---

Sir, In 1943, when I took over the inventory of the RAF Hospital in Reykjavik, I had to sign for one item entitled: 'Bedpans, rubber, lunatics for the use of'.

*The Times, October 1982*

Sir, As a newly-commissioned officer in 1940, I was intrigued to find that in our makeshift accommodation my colleagues and I would be credited 'Field Allowance' of 2s/- daily by the Paymaster if the Quartermaster was unable to supply us with the officially prescribed essentials of furnishing, viz,

One coal scuttle (officer's),
One poker (soldier's),
One chair (Windsor or fold-flat),
One inventory board.

As we were accommodated outdoors in bell tents, the likely usefulness of the first two items was as baffling as the apparent class distinction between them. Fortunately for us, however, they were in short supply and so we got our 2s/- daily to compensate. However, the Quartermaster was able to provide the chair – thus saving himself the ignominy of issuing an inventory board with nothing listed upon it except itself.

*The Times, October 1982*

Sir, That dogs of all breeds and sizes are musical is generally known and agreed; but the reason they are unable to carry their talents further has been overlooked by your correspondents.

Dogs lack rhythm: What, after all, is the difference between a howl and a note but the question of knowing when to stop? Dogs, in common with Italian prima donnas, are inclined to hang on to a good thing. It is not that they cannot hit the note, but that they do not know when to come off it. They have not, like Mussolini, learned the value of the 'Indispensable pause'. They have tone, they have colour; they understand the glissando and the tremolo; some have fine lungs and a good ear (I once knew a bitch with absolute pitch); but, Sir, they cannot master the 3:4 nor the 6:8.

Now the horse can waltz. The snake, though science assures us it is deaf, will move its hips at the lure of the flageolet. The sea lion, as visitors to Olympia will observe, has 'rhythm in a great big way' and can syncopate and shimmy with the best hula from Havana. But the dog, the friend of man – alas, it is a sobering thought – cannot, after years of broadcast jazz, master the blues.

No doubt your columns could be filled for weeks with diverse instances

of the canine love of the vocal line; but will anyone come forward and claim they have a dog with rhythm? Should the phenomenon exist, vistas of possibilities blossom. Such a creature, under expert tutelage might acquire taps, routines, and breaks that, having four legs and a tail to accomplish them with, might astonish the world.

Darwin played the trumpet to a row of runner beans to see if music would affect their growth. He was unable to detect any reaction; but who knows? Such things, in this age of surprising discoveries, should be investigated. Will no one give a poodle to Fred Astaire?

Yours faithfully,
Cecil Lewis

January 1936

***Cecil Lewis** (1898-1997), First World War air ace as a teenager; one of the five founders of the BBC; and, in 1938, co-winner with George Bernard Shaw of an Oscar for the script of 'Pygmalion'. Military Cross in Second World War. 'You should live gloriously, generously, dangerously', he wrote in his memoir. 'The Prince of Pilots, a Master of Words and a bit of a poet' – GBS. Married in Peking, Evdekia Horvath, the 18 year old daughter of an Imperial Russian general (their only common language was French)*

Sir, It started off well. Only a few months after I succeeded to my father's title, I handed over my shiny new passport – in which the prefix 'The Right Honourable', was written out in full – to the receptionist at the Sion Hotel, Llubljiana, and was duly inscribed in his register as the one thing I had always wanted to be: Mr Right.

Since then, however, I have gone steadily downhill. There was a bad moment some years ago when another receptionist, ashen-faced, handed me a sinister-looking envelope on which I was addressed as The Vice Count; but even then the depths were not yet plumbed. The ultimate – I hope – humiliation came only quite recently, when I received a missive addressed to me – in the style according to which I now sign myself – as: Your obedient servant, The Discount Norwich.

John Julius Norwich January 1982

***John Julius Norwich, Viscount Norwich***

Sir, The tale of the Wykehamist and the chair (the Wykehamist offers the chair, the Etonian fetches it and the Harrovian sits on it) calls to mind the anecdote illustrating the distinguishing characteristics of the five Oxford 'women's' colleges.

Five girls, one from each college, meet. Their conversation concerns a young man of their mutual acquaintance.

The girl from Lady Margaret Hall asks, 'Who are his parents?'

The girl from Somerville asks, 'What is he reading?'

The girl from St Hugh's asks, 'What sport does he play?'

The girl from St Hilda's asks, 'Who is he going out with?'

And the girl from St Anne's says, 'Me'.

At least, that is the version which I was told, when I was at St Anne's.

Yours faithfully,

Imogen Clout

*From 'Great Letters: A century of notable correspondence', 2017.*
*450 letters from 1914-2014*

The trouble with an orgy is that you don't know who to thank.

***Bob Monkhouse** (1928-2003), writer, comedian, actor.*
*Serial sexual participant.*

Last night I ordered an entire meal in French, and even the waiter was surprised. It was a Chinese restaurant.

***Tommy Cooper** (1921-1984), comedian and magician.*
*'The tightest man in show business' – John Fisher*

Doing business without advertising is like winking at a girl in the dark. You know what you are doing, but nobody else does.

***Steuart Henderson Britt** (1907-1979), American psychologist and professor of marketing*

I'll beat him so bad he'll need a shoehorn to put his hat on.

***Muhammad Ali** (born Cassius Marcellus Clay) (1942-2016),*
*American professional boxer. Philanthropist and activist.*
*21 World Heavyweight titles. Married four times, nine children*

I like to do all the talking myself. It saves time and prevents arguments.

***Oscar Wilde** (1854-1900), Irish poet and playwright*

When they come down from their Ivory Towers,
Idealists are apt to walk straight into the gutter.

*Truly miscellaneous:*

- * Ostriches stick their heads in the sand to look for water.
- * English is second only to Mandarin in number of speakers.
- * A giraffe can clean its ears with its 21-inch tongue.
- * The grizzly bear can run as fast as the average horse.
- * Eskimos use refrigerators to keep food from freezing.

*From the 1500s:*

* The phrase 'rule of thumb' is derived from an old English law, which stated that you couldn't beat your wife with anything wider than your thumb.

* Most people got married in June because they took their yearly bath in May. If they started to smell the bride carried a bouquet of sweet smelling flowers. The custom still exists.

* Baths were taken in a big tub with the man of the house having the first with clean water. Next were the sons, followed by the women and finally the children. By this time the water might be so dirty a baby could be lost in it. Hence the saying 'Don't throw the baby out with the bath water'.

* Floors of the poor were dirt, hence the saying 'Dirt poor'. The slate floors of the wealthy could get slippery in winter. Thresh was added until it got too much and started to slip outside; a piece of wood was then placed in the entranceway – 'a thresh hold'.

* Thatched roofs were piled high with straw and were a place where animals could keep warm. When it rained, the straw got slippery and animals lost their foothold and fell out, hence the saying 'It's raining cats and dogs'.

---

The largest tyre producer in the world is LEGO.

Style is when they're running you out of town and you make it look as if you're leading a parade.

***William Battie** (1703-1776), English physician*

Opera is where a guy gets stabbed in the back and, instead of bleeding, he sings.

***Ed Gardner** (b 1974), conductor, choral scholar, musician*

Flattery is like chewing gum. Enjoy it, but don't swallow it.

***Hank Ketcham** (1920-2001), American cartoonist, creator of Dennis the Menace*

A man who can drive safely while kissing a pretty girl is simply not giving the kiss the attention it deserves.

***Albert Einstein** (1879-1955), Jewish German theoretical physicist. Nobel Prize for Physics. Acquired both Swiss and American citizenship. Violinist*

When a man sits with a pretty girl for an hour, it seems like a minute. But let him sit on a hot stove for a minute – and it seems longer than an hour. That's relativity.

*Ibid*

Being an astronomer is a very noble profession, but it does leave you at rather a loose end during the day.

***Sir Patrick Caldwell-Moore** (1923-2012), astronomer, television presenter. Xylophonist. Author. Airman*

*Mark Twain's,* 'A lie is halfway round the world before the truth has got its boots on', *is now taken as an instruction.*

*Bodie – a town so lawless that in 1881 it was described as* '… a sea of sin, lashed by the tempests of lust and passion'.

***Reverend FM Warrington.*** *65 saloons in a town of 8,000*

The road to success is always under construction.

***Arnold Palmer*** *(1929-2016), American professional golfer. 62 PGA titles. Pilot and car dealer*

I'm a wonderful housekeeper. Every time I get a divorce, I keep the house.

***Zsa Zsa Gabor*** *(1917-2016), Hungarian/American actress and socialite. Nine husbands. One daughter and ten adopted sons*

*When asked if she had posed for a calendar with nothing on,* ***Marilyn Monroe*** *(1926-1962) replied,* 'I had the radio on'.

*A note left on the windscreen:*

Dearest Warden. Front tooth broken off: look like 81-year-old pirate, so at dentist, 19a. Very old, very lame – no meter money.

***Lady Diana Cooper****, Viscountess Norwich (1892-1986), wife of Duff Cooper. Member of the Coterie. Socialite and intellectual*

---

I rang for ice, but this is ridiculous.

***Madeleine Astor*** *(born Madeleine Talmage Force Fiermonte) (1893-1940), American socialite. Second wife of John Jacob Astor IV. Her last comment on leaving the Titanic. Titanic survivor*

I would like to throw an egg into an electric fan.

***Joyce Grenfell*** *(1910-1979), comedienne, singer, actress, monologist when asked for her ultimate ambition*

If you're going to say anything filthy, please speak clearly after the tone.

***Viv Stanshall*** *(1943-1955), musician, poet. Member of Bonzo Dog Doo-Dah Band. Message on her telephone answering machine*

Well, if I called the wrong number, why did you answer the phone?

***James Thurber** (1894-1961), American cartoonist, author, playwright. Caption in The New Yorker, June 1937.*

Have you noticed that wrong numbers are never engaged?

*Retorts:*

'Have a nice day' – 'I've got other plans.'

'No problem' – 'I wasn't expecting any.'

***Peter Ustinov** (1921-2004), actor, writer, film maker. 102 films. 34 published writings*

---

*Spectatum veniunt, veniunt spectentur.*
[They come to look and be looked at.]

***Publius Ovidius Naso**, known as Ovid. (43BC-17AD)*

*Quidris recte factum; quamvis humile praeclarum*
[Whatsoever is rightly done, however humble, is noble]

*Rolls-Royce motto*

*Braille:*

In 1824, the French army captain, Charles Barbier de la Serre, invented the basic technique of using raised dots for tactile writing and reading to allow soldiers to compose and read messages at night without light.

Each braille cell is made up of six dot positions, which are arranged in a rectangle comprising two columns of three dots. A dot may be raised at any one of the six positions, and in any combination. Counting the space – where no dots are raised – there are 64 combinations.

---

Borrow money from pessimists – they don't expect it back.

We are living in a world today where lemonade is made from artificial flavours and furniture polish is made from real lemons.

***Alfred Newman*** *(1900-1970), American composer and conductor. 44 Oscar nominations for film scores*

Q: How did you get out of Iraq?
A: Iran

Only the Americans have mastered the art of being prosperous though insolvent.

One of the lessons of history is that nothing is often a good thing to do and always a clever thing to say.

***William Durant** (1861-1947), co-founder of General Motors and Frigidaire. Later pioneered bowling alleys. American engineer*

The right most valued by all civilised men is the right to be left alone.

***Louis Dembitz Brandeis** (1856-1941), American lawyer and Justice of Supreme Court. Born of Polish Ashkenazi immigrant Jews*

Whatever you do, kid, always serve it with a little dressing.

***George M Cohan** (1878-1942), American entertainer, composer, singer, dancer*

Sir, I read with interest the letter from Simon Pike. I believe my father, Canon William Barnard, was perhaps the first to hold an animal service, in his church at Hinton Martell, near Wimborne Minster, in 1954; a service has been held annually ever since. Celebrities such as Spike Milligan, James Mason and Leslie Crowther spoke at the service over the years. Even though dogs are banned from the grounds of Sherborne Abbey, Bishop Pike would no doubt be pleased to learn they are still welcomed at Salisbury Cathedral, where I am head guide; only yesterday I had a long conversation with two Pyrenean mountain dogs in the north transept.

***Christopher Barnard**, Verwood, Dorset*

I sympathise with Bernard Levin's negative view of Debussy's opera Pelléas et Mélisande. I collect pithy dismissals of composers inclined to take themselves too seriously. Tchaikovsky called Wagner's Ring Cycle 'this boring . . . spun-out yarn'. Thomas Adés has accused Mahler of producing 'cheap, automatic trash' and George Bernard Shaw said that A German Requiem by Brahms 'is patiently borne only by the corpse'.

*The Times*

Whoever scatters thorns should not go around shoeless.

*Neapolitan Mafioso, quoted in The Times*

'Diamonds Are Forever' was a direct lift from the De Beers advertising slogan dreamed up by copywriter Frances Gerety in 1947.

'You Only Live Twice' was a phrase coined by the 17th-century Japanese poet Matsuo Basho.

Ian Fleming's lover in later life, Blanche de Blockwell, gave him a small boat which she named 'Octopussy'; this became the name of a man-eating pet octopus in the short story.

Of those to whom much is given, much is required. And when at some future date the high court of history sits in judgment on each of us... recording whether in our brief span of service we fulfilled our responsibilities... our success or failure, we will be measured by the answers to four questions: Were we men of courage? Were we truly men of judgment? Were we truly men of integrity? Were we truly men of dedication?

***John F Kennedy** (1917-1963), 35th President of United States.*
*Assassinated 22nd November 1963*

According to legend, Pablo Escobar (born Pablo Gaviria) (1949-1993), the Colombian drug baron who once supplied 80% of the world's cocaine, spent $2,500 per month on the elastic bands needed to hold his cash. The narcoterrorist was founder of the Medelin Cartel which smuggled 80 tons of cocaine into the United States each month. Personal wealth of $48 billion.

*The writer and socialite Taki described Bob Geldof, at one time the treasurer of the Pugs Club, as having short arms and deep pockets.* 'A suitable role for a man whose idea of an unnatural act is to reach for the bill.'

***Panagiotis Theodoracopulos, 'Taki'*** *(b 1936), Greek journalist, skiing and tennis champion. Black belt in karate.*

***Sir Robert Zenon 'Bob' Geldof*** *(b 1951), Irish singer songwriter, author, political activist. Organiser of Live Aid charity event.*

*In the United States in1920 – just 100 years ago:*

- The average life expectancy for a man was 47 years.
- Fuel for the popular Ford Model T was sold only in drug stores.
- There was no radio or TV.
- Only 14% of homes had a bath.
- Only 8% of homes had a telephone.
- There were only 144 miles of paved roads.
- The maximum speed limit in most cities was 10mph.
- The tallest structure in the world was the Eiffel Tower.
- Most women washed their hair once a month and used Borax or egg yolks for shampoo.
- The five leading causes of death were pneumonia; influenza; tuberculosis (consumption); diarrhoea; heart disease.
- The population of Las Vegas was only 30.
- There was no Mother's Day or Father's Day.

*... and in another 100 years?*

BENEATH THIS STONE RESTS THE BODY
OF A BRITISH WARRIOR
UNKNOWN BY NAME OR RANK
BROUGHT FROM FRANCE TO LIE AMONG
THE MOST ILLUSTRIOUS OF THE LAND
AND BURIED HERE ON ARMISTICE DAY
11 NOV: 1920 IN THE PRESENCE OF
HIS MAJESTY KING GEORGE V
HIS MINISTERS OF STATE
THE CHIEFS OF HIS FORCES
AND A VAST CONCOURSE OF THE NATION

THUS ARE COMMEMORATED THE MANY
MULTITUDES WHO DURING THE GREAT
WAR OF 1914-1918 GAVE THE MOST THAT
MAN CAN GIVE LIFE ITSELF
FOR GOD
FOR KING AND COUNTRY
FOR LOVED ONES HOME AND EMPIRE
FOR THE SACRED CAUSE OF JUSTICE AND
THE FREEDOM OF THE WORLD

THEY BURIED HIM AMONG THE KINGS BECAUSE HE
HAD DONE GOOD TOWARD GOD AND TOWARD
HIS HOUSE

UNKNOWN YET WELL KNOWN
IN CHRIST SHALL ALL BE MADE ALIVE

*The Tomb of the Unknown Warrior, Westminster Abbey*

**Peerage in Britain and Ireland**

| | |
|---|---|
| 31 | Dukes & Duchesses |
| 34 | Marquesses & Marchionesses |
| 193 | Earls & Countesses |
| 112 | Viscounts & Viscountesses |
| 1,187 | Barons & Baronesses |

**Peerage in Scotland**

| | |
|---|---|
| 9 | Dukes & Duchesses |
| 16 | Marquesses |
| 81 | Earls |
| 38 | Viscounts |
| 109 | Lords & Ladies |

There are also Baronetcies, Hereditary Knights, Dames, Clan Chiefs, Lairds and Esquires.

*Current orders of chivalry, in order of precedence:*

| | |
|---|---|
| 1348 | The Most Noble Order of the Garter |
| 1687 | The Most Ancient and Most Noble Order of the Thistle |
| 1725 | The Most Honourable Order of the Bath |
| 1902 | Order of Merit |
| 1818 | The Most Distinguished Order of Saint Michael and Saint George |
| 1886 | The Distinguished Service Order |
| 1896 | The Royal Victorian Order |
| 1917 | The Most Excellent Order of the British Empire |
| 1917 | The Order of the Companions of Honour |

**The Archbishop of Canterbury** is the 'Supreme Governor' of the Church and the highest ranking non-royal in the United Kingdom's order of precedence. He is the diocesan bishop of the Diocese of Canterbury and Metropolitan Archbishop of the Province of Canterbury (this covers the southern two thirds of England). He signs his name 'Cantuar' (the Latin for Canterbury).

The title of **Earl Marshal** is always held by the Duke of Norfolk of the day. He is responsible for Coronations, State Funerals and the State Opening of Parliament. He also presides over the College of Arms and grants armorial bearings.

The three Kings or Arms are: Garter (blue)
Clarenceux
Norroy and Ulster

The four Pursuivants are: Rouge Dragon
Bluemantle
Portcullis
Rouge Croix

The six Heralds are styled: Somerset Herald
Richmond Herald
Lancaster Herald
Windsor Herald
Chester Herald
York Herald

*The Great Officers Of State, in order of precedence after the Royal family:*

Archbishop of Canterbury
(The Lord High Steward – vacant since 1421)
Lord High Chancellor
Lord High Treasurer
Lord President of the Council
Lord Keeper of the Privy Seal
Lord Great Chamberlain
Lord High Constable
Earl Marshal
Lord High Admiral

*Holders of archaic titles who wait upon the sovereign on certain state occasions include:*

Garter Principal King of Arms
The Lord President of the Council
Keeper of Her Majesty's Purse
Gentleman Usher to Her Majesty
The Comptroller of Her Majesty's Household
Treasurer of Her Majesty's Household
Keeper of Her Majesty's Privy Purse
Equerry in Waiting to Her Majesty
The Lord Privy Seal
The Gentleman Usher of the Black Rod
The Master of the Horse
The Lord Steward
The Mistress of the Robes
The Lady of the Bedchamber
The Goldstick in Waiting
The Queen's Champion
The Silver Stick in Waiting
The Field Officer in Brigade Waiting
Comptroller of the Lord Chamberlain's Office
Gentleman Usher to the Sword of State
Captain of the Corps of Gentlemen at Arms
Captain of the Yeoman of the Guard
The First and Principal Naval Aide-de-Camp to Her Majesty
Aide-de-Camp General to Her Majesty

There are 98 named positions within the British Royal Household.

*On the night of 5/6th February 1952 King George VI died in his sleep at Sandringham:*

During these last months the King walked with death, as if death were a companion, an acquaintance, whom he recognised and did not fear. In the end death came as a friend; and after a happy day of sunshine and sport, and after 'good night' to those who loved him best, he fell asleep as every man or woman who strives to fear God and nothing else in the world may hope to do...

***Sir Winston Churchill** (1874-1965)*

---

*Remembering Roy Brooks, the honest estate agent:*

£5,995 FHLD! Broken-down Battersea Bargain. Erected at end of long reign of increasingly warped moral & aesthetic values it's what you expect – hideous; redeemed only by the integrity of the plebs who built it – well. Originally a one skiv Victorian lower-middle class fmly res, it'll probably be snapped up by one of the new Communications Elite, who'll tart it up & flog it for 15 thou. 3 normal-sized bedrms & a 4th for an undemanding dwarf lodger, Bathrm. Big dble drawing rm. B'fast rm & kit. Nature has fought back in the gdn – & won. Call Sun 3-5 at 21 Surrey Lane, S.W.11, then Brooks.

*Roy Brooks, who died in 1971, was an estate agent in Kings Road, London who made his name and, uncomfortably for a man with avowed communistic leanings, his fortune from harnessing one endearing feature into the prose eschewed by other estate agents of the time – the unvarnished truth. Who could resist making an appointment to view a bargain described thus:*

> Wanted: Someone with taste, means and a stomach strong enough to buy this erstwhile house of ill-repute in Pimlico. It is untouched by the 20th century as far as conveniences for even the basic human decencies are concerned. Although it reeks of damp or worse, the plaster is coming off the walls and daylight peeps through a hole in the roof, it is still habitable judging by the bed of rags, fag ends and empty bottles in one corner. Plenty of scope for the socially aspiring to express their decorative taste and get their abode in The Glossy, and nothing to stop them putting Westminster on their notepaper. Comprises 10 rather unpleasant rooms with slimy back yard, £4,650 Freehold. Tarted up, these houses make £15,000.

*Or:*

> Do not be misled by the trim exterior of this modest period res with its dirty broken windows; all is not well with the inside. The decor of the nine rooms, some of which hangs inelegantly from the walls, is revolting. Not entirely devoid of plumbing, there is a pathetic kitchen and one cold tap. No bathroom, of course, but Chelsea has excellent public baths. Rain sadly drips through the ceiling on to the oilcloth. The pock-marked basement floor indicates a thriving community of woodworm, otherwise there is not much wrong with the property... Sacrifice £6,750.

*Becoming wealthy from the enormous fees thrown at him by London's upper crust (5% on the first £500, 2.5% on the next £4,500 and 1.5% on the residue) never sat comfortably with this surprisingly socially conscious agent.*

*Roy Brooks would occasionally load his Rolls-Royce with 1,000 pairs of shoes and drive to Russia with them, saying:* 'I take these for old times' sake.'

*Legislation such as the Property Misdescriptions Act would probably rule out a return to such outlandish frankness today but if it's true, decent and honest it can't be illegal, can it?*

---

Sir, The death of John Hay Whitney, whose obituary you publish today, enables me to relieve my conscience of a burden it has been carrying for almost two decades, and I would be grateful if you would allow me, in your columns, to make open confession – so good, they say, for the soul.

Not long after, in 1961, Whitney bought the New York Herald Tribune, I was visiting that city and having lunch with a friend who worked on the paper. I called at his office to pick him up, and as we had some time in hand, he offered to show me round the building. Eventually we got to the executive floor (if you think you have a posh executive floor at The Times, and indeed posh executives, you should have seen the ones at the Trib) and my friend, with the insouciance of a man who knows the back way in to Fort Knox, ushered me into Whitney's office (the boss was out to lunch, you see).

I sank up to my collar in the carpet, and eventually, hacking my way through the undergrowth, came to a desk about the size of Victoria Station. On it there was nothing but a blotter-pad, some tastefully-arranged pencils, and a green eyeshade.

Now you and I know, of course, that newspapermen do not wear green eyeshades except in bad films; presumably, however, nobody had told Mr Whitney this (well, you wouldn't tell Mr Murdoch if his shirt was hanging out, would you?), and there the thing was. It was an exceptionally up-market green eyeshade, I may say, made out of some very firm Perspex-type plastic, and with a beautiful padded strip round the top to avoid chafing the boss's forehead or temples.

The ink blushes red in my pen as I write the words, but write them I must. Sir, madness swept over me, the high principles by which I had always endeavoured to guide my life vanished in an instant, and Belial had me in his grip. I determined to steal John Hay Whitney's green eyeshade.

With the last vestiges of decency that remained to me, I bade my friend turn his back, so that he could truthfully say, when the uproar started, that he had seen nothing untoward take place. I then tucked the green eyeshade under my jackets, and we went to lunch.

Ever since, the guilt of that crime has dogged me, day and night. But I must expiate it at last, if only because Whitney may even now be explaining to his Maker that he ought to be let off a good deal of Purgatory because his life had been soured by the theft of his green eyeshade, and that his Maker ought to be going after the villain who had nicked it instead of him.

I feel better already. I have to add, though, that when I left the paper on which we then both worked, I bequeathed the green eyeshade of John Hay Whitney to Katharine Whitehorn. As far as I know, she has never lost a moment's sleep over her role as an accessory after the fact. But that is her problem now.

My best wishes to you all down there. I bet Mr Murdoch doesn't wear a green eyeshade. Ta-ta for now.
February 1982

***Bernard Levin** (1928-2004), author, broadcaster and journalist – Taper column in Spectator followed by The Times.18 published works.*

## ECCENTRICS

*To my mind, life is immeasurably enhanced by eccentric personalities and eccentric episodes. Consider:*

* John Christie (1882-1962), the originator of the Glyndebourne Opera Festival. He had a glass eye (famously taken out and polished in front of the Queen), wore lederhosen, travelled third class and refused porterage to save tipping.

* Sir George Sitwell (1860-1943), father of the only mildly eccentric Edith Sitwell, tried to pay his son's Eton school fees with fresh produce from his estate, decorated his cows and in his house disallowed any contradiction to his views. For recreation he shot wasps with his revolver.

* Gerald Tyrwhitt-Wilson (1883-1950), Lord Berners, dyed his pigeons in several colours, had a pet giraffe to have tea with, and adapted his Rolls-Royce to accommodate a clavichord (he was an accomplished pianist).

* Francis Egerton, 8th Earl of Bridgewater (1756-1829), was famous for his dinner parties for favourite dogs.

*Here is Ben Macintyre from a piece in The Times of March 2019:*

The British army itself, however, has probably produced more eccentrics than any other national institution, with the exception of the aristocracy. Take the one-eyed general Sir Adrian Paul Ghislain Carton de Wiart, VC, who fought in the Boer, First and Second World Wars, suffered wounds to the face, head, stomach, hip, legs and ear, survived two plane crashes, tunnelled out of a POW camp, and ripped off his own fingers because a doctor declined to amputate. When he fell down the stairs in Rangoon and knocked himself out at the age of 68, surgeons took the opportunity to remove some of the bits of shrapnel still lying around his body.

For truly world-class eccentricity few could equal Rev Dr Joseph Wolff, an Anglican vicar born in 1795 who set off on a lifelong odyssey across the Middle East, central Asia and the Caucasus on a mission to convert the heathen and find the ten lost tribes of Israel. Along the way, he argued with Christians, Jews, Hindus, Sunnis and Shias. The consequences were frequently unpleasant. Bandits tied him to the tail of a horse, he was stripped naked three times and came close to being burnt alive.

***Benedict Macintyre** (b 1963), historian, journalist, author.*
*Fourteen published works, fourteen literary awards*

---

The poor are like stars in the dark of the night.

***Imelda Marcos** (born Imelda Romualdez) (b 1929), First Lady of The Philippines. Reputedly had 3,000 pairs of shoes. Known for her extravagance*

*To the President of Nigeria, dressed in traditional robes:*
You look like you're ready for bed.

*When asked if he would like to visit the Soviet Union:*
The bastards murdered half my family.

*To a student who had been trekking in Papua, New Guinea:*
You managed not to get eaten, then?

***Prince Philip, Duke of Edinburgh** (b 1921),*
*Patron of 780 organisations*

An improper mind is a perpetual feast.

***Oscar Wilde*** *(1854-1900), Irish poet and playwright*

*Lord Northcliffe:* 'Looking at how thin you are, people would think there was a famine in England.
*George Bernard Shaw:* 'And looking at how fat you are, people would think you were the cause of it.'

***Alfred Harmsworth, 11th Viscount Northcliffe*** *(1865-1922), newspaper magnate. Initiated Harmsworth Cup for powerboat racing*

*On Arianna Stassinopoulos:*

So boring you fall asleep halfway through her name.

*Arianna Stassinopoulos (b 1950), Greek/American author and columnist. Founder of Huffington Post*

I'm amazed he was such a good shot.

***Sir Noël Coward*** *(1899-1973), playwright, composer, actor, singer. On being told that his accountant had blown his brains out.*

*When Noel Coward was asked why he had champagne for breakfast, he replied,* "Doesn't everyone?"

# 9 | Wordplay and Numbers

*Punctuation best demonstrated. Eighty four word sentence and entirely comprehensible:*

> Sir, Mrs Carter-Ruck writes nostalgically of the old-fashioned box camera, but can anything match the sense of impotence which overcame one when, expecting the 1 in the little red window, one encountered the 2, and realized that, arrangements for rewinding the film being rigorously excluded from such devices, presumably lest they confuse the untutored, an eighth of one's film was, whilst in principle as ready as ever to receive the image of one's choice, in practice irretrievably lost?
> Canterbury, Kent

*The Times, April 1983*

How is it possible to have a civil war?

***George Carlin*** *(1937-2008), American actor, comedian and author*

The common speech of the Commonwealth of Australia represents the most brutal maltreatment which has ever been inflicted upon the mother-tongue of the great English-speaking nations.

*__Sir Winston Churchill__ (1874-1965),*
*British Prime Minister 1940-1945*

Australia is the only country in the world where the word 'academic' is regularly used as a term of abuse.

*__Dame Leonie Kramer__ (1924-2016), Australian academic.*
*First female professor of English in Australia*

Slang is language that takes off its coat, rolls up its sleeves, spits on its hands, and goes to work.

*__Carl Sandberg__ (1878-1967), American poet and biographer.*
*Three Pulitzer Prizes. Ardent supporter of Civil Rights Movement*

*Anagrams of well known names:*

Osama Bin Laden . . . . . . . . . . . . . .A bad man (no lies)
The terrorist Osama Bin Laden . . . .Arab monster is no idle threat
Margaret Thatcher . . . . . . . . . . . . .That great charmer
Clint Eastwood . . . . . . . . . . . . . . . .Old West action
Leonardo da Vinci. . . . . . . . . . . . . .Did color in a nave
Nurse Florence Nightingale. . . . . . .Heroine curing fallen gents
William Shakespeare . . . . . . . . . . . .I am a weakish speller
. . . . . . . . . . . . . . . . . . . . . . . . . . .I'll make a wise phrase

*...and the longest?*

That's one small step for a man, one giant leap for mankind – Neil Armstrong . . . . . . . .A thin man ran, makes large stride, pins flag on moon, left planet – on to Mars.

***Imogen Skirving*** *(1937-2016), hotelier of Langar Hall,* 'an 8-foot personality in a 5-foot frame' *had a penchant for anagrams. These are some of her best:*

Astronomer.................... Moon starer
Election results ................ Lies – let's recount
Eleven plus two................ Twelve plus one
Slot machines ................. Cash lost in me
The eyes ...................... They see

*Just before the first print run of Under Milk Wood, Dylan Thomas altered the name of his Welsh fishing village from Llareggub to Llareggyb. He suddenly realised that, when reversed, the original name spelled* 'Buggerall'.

> Surely to tell these tall tales and others like them would be to speed the myth, the wicked lie, that the past is always tense and the future perfect.

***Zadie Smith*** *(b 1975), novelist and short story writer.*
*From 'White Teeth' (2000), her debut novel.*
*Auctioned for rights when only part written*

*Advice for a gardener:*

Grow PEAS of mind
LETTUCE be thankful
SQUASH selfishness
TURNIP to help
and always
Make THYME for loved ones

*Sign in the garden of Oberoi Hotel, Mauritius*

MISSING MAN FOUND IN SANDWICH

Why do the French only have one egg for breakfast?
Because one egg is *un oeuf*.

*Similes are staple ingredients in a writer's larder. Many authors are well known for their imaginative similes. Here are just four:*

*PG Wodehouse*

Small, shrivelled chap, like a haddock with lung troubles.

Lady Constance looks on me as a sort of cross between a leper and a nosegay of deadly nightshade.

Aunt Agatha, who eats broken bottles and wears barbed wire next to her skin.

*Raymond Chandler*

Blank expression, like a farm boy at a Latin lesson.

As careful as an out of work showgirl in her last pair of good stockings.

Neck like a cartoon Prussian corporal.

Smooth as a bandleader's hair.

Thinner than the gold of a weekend wedding ring.

*Dorothy Parker*

Bristling like a terrier spotting a postman.

*Oscar Wilde*

So dreadfully dowdy she reminded one of a badly worn hymn book.

- The number 2,520 can be divided by 1, 2, 3, 4, 5, 6 7, 8, 9 and 10.
- The numbers 111, 222, 333, 444, 555, 666, 777, 888, 999 are all multiples of 37.
- The Mariana Trench, the deepest in all the world's oceans, located south-east of Japan, has a depth of 11,035 metres; by comparison the height of Mount Everest is only 8,884 metres.
- The world spends over $2 billion a day on weaponry.
- Earth's closest star in the Milky Way, *Proxima Centauri*, is more than four light-years away – a light-year being about 5.9 trillion miles or about 10 trillion kilometres. *Proxima* is Latin for 'close'.

Pythagoras' Theorem: . . . . . . . . . . . . . . . . . . . . . .24 words
The Lord's Prayer: . . . . . . . . . . . . . . . . . . . . . . .66 words
Ten Commandments: . . . . . . . . . . . . . . . . . . . . .179 words
Gettysburg Address: . . . . . . . . . . . . . . . . . . . . .286 words
US Declaration of Independence: . . . . . . . . . 1,300 words
US Constitution with all 27 Amendments:. . . 7,818 words
EU regulations on the sale of cabbages: . . . . 26,911 words

*These numbers can be found in the 15th century Cathedral of the Holy Cross in Barcelona:*

| | | | |
|---|---|---|---|
| 1 | 14 | 14 | 4 |
| 11 | 7 | 6 | 9 |
| 8 | 10 | 10 | 5 |
| 13 | 2 | 3 | 15 |

*All lines horizontally, vertically and diagonally add up to 33. Christ lived 33 years.*

Statistics are like bikinis. What they reveal is suggestive but what they conceal is vital.

***Aaron Levenstein** (1913-1986), American statistician*

*The English language has always had a reputation for being difficult to learn and it is uniquely difficult to correctly pronounce. Consider:*

The wind was too strong to wind in the sail.
I had to subject that subject to tests.
Too close to a door to close it.
A bandage was wound around the wound.
The invalid had invalid insurance.
There was no time like the present to present the present.

*There are many more to confuse.*

*Then, there are paradoxes to further confound:*

A slim chance and a fat chance are similar.
But a wise man and a wise guy are opposites.
Cat gut comes from sheep or horses.
You can burn down a house as it burns up.
While filling out a form, you fill it in.
The alarm goes off by going on.
Ecuador makes Panama hats.
A purple finch is red.
No egg in an eggplant.
No ham in a hamburger.
Neither apple nor pine in a pineapple.
Boxing rings are square.

*The theory of Nominative Determinisim (people with an appropriate name for their job) was coined in an article in New Scientist in 1994 about the urologists Splatt and Weedon. The Times had played this game twenty years earlier when The Diary noted that Inspector Barker was head of the dogs' section of Merseyside. Since then The Diary and its letters' pages have produced many more of these appropriate name. In 2002 The Journal of Personality and Social Psychology published research into Implicit Egotism that suggested that people's names influenced their careers. The remarkable truth is that all these that follow do or have existed.*

| | |
|---|---|
| *Legal* | Igor Judge – Lord Chief Justice |
| | John Laws – Lord Justice of Appeal |
| | Jennifer Justice – lawyer |
| *Medical* | Dr Richard Chopp – vasectomy consultant |
| | Dr Richard Brain – neurologist |
| | Dr Randall Toothaker – dental surgeon |
| | Shaun McCracken – chiropractor |
| | Dr Ashley Seawright – optician |
| | Lee Breakwell – orthopaedic surgeon |
| *Sport* | Prince Fielder – baseball |
| | Usain Bolt – athletics |
| | Scott Speed – car racing |
| | Maria Stepanova – hurdles |
| | Anna Smashnova – tennis |
| *Also* | Carla Dove – ornithologist |
| | Mitchell Byrd – ornithologist |
| | Amy Freeze – meteorologist |
| | Storm Field – meteorologist |
| | Marietta Clinkscales – piano teacher |
| | Anna & Frank Webb – arachnologists |
| | Brad Slaughter – butcher |
| | Robin Banks – policeman |
| | Donald Buttress – surveyor to Westminster Abbey |
| | Susan Tugwell – midwife |
| | Freddie Garland – florist |

*Amazingly, the following firms are trading or have done so:*

| | |
|---|---|
| *Solicitors* | Argue & Phibbs |
| | Stoneham, Bircham & Hangem |
| | Welsh & Robb |
| | Sue, Grabbit & Runne |
| *Also* | Nott & Earthly – turf accountants |
| | Gowin, Gowin and Gonn – auctioneers |
| | Nasher, Fang and Fillingham – dental practice |
| | Doolittle and Dalley – estate agents |

---

## *Oxymorons*

*In its Greek origin,* αιχμηρός *(sharp) was combined with* αμβλύς *(dull) to give* Οξύμωρο. *These apparently contradictory terms have been cleverly exploited by writers, such as Tennyson's* 'And faith unfaithful kept him falsely true' *and provided amusement for readers with very many examples. These are a few:*

Act naturally
Found missing
Advanced BASIC
Genuine imitation
Good grief
Almost exactly
Deafening silence
Living dead
Business ethics
Sweet sorrow
Tight slacks
Jumbo shrimps
Plastic glasses
Random order
Original copy
Pretty ugly
Diet ice-cream
Working holiday

*There are hundreds more.*

*Many oxymorons are unintentional and the most famous proponent of these accidental but fortuitous slips was Samuel Goldwyn. Like these:*

- A verbal contract isn't worth the paper it's written on
- If I could drop dead right now, I'd be the happiest man alive
- It's more than magnificent, it's mediocre
- If Roosevelt was alive he'd turn over in his grave
- I'll give you an absolute maybe
- If you fall and break your legs, don't come running to me
- I don't think anyone should write their autobiography until they're dead
- Spare no expense to save money on this
- Tell him to put more life into his dying

***Samuel Goldwyn** (aka Samuel Goldfish, born Szmuel Gelbfisz) (1879-1974), Polish glove salesman. Hollywood film producer of 51 films. Presidential Medal of Freedom*

# 10 | Food and Drink

We may live without poetry, music and art;
We may live without conscience and live without heart;
We may live without friends; we may live without books;
But civilised man cannot live without cooks.

***Owen Meredith (pseudonym of Edward Bulwer-Lytton, 1st Earl Lytton)** (1831-1894), statesman, politician and poet. Viceroy of India*

The human digestive system is between 26 and 33 feet long.

The stomach contains hydrochloric acid. It must produce a layer of mucus regularly (every two weeks) or it will digest itself.

An AGA stove was originally called a Aktienbolage Gasaccumulator.

A cucumber should be well sliced and dressed with pepper and salt and then thrown out as good for nothing.

***Samuel Johnson (Dr Johnson)** (1709-1784), poet, playwright, biographer, lexicographer. Author of first English Dictionary*

The most remarkable thing about my mother is that for 30 years she served the family only leftovers. The original meal has never been found.

***Sam Levenson** (1911-1980), American humourist and television host*

There are two things I like firm and one of them is jelly.

***Mary Jane 'Mae' West** (1893-1980), American actress, singer, comedienne and sex symbol*

There is no light so perfect as that which shines from an open fridge door at 2am.

***Nigel Slater** (b 1958), food writer and journalist. 16 cook books*

The fact is, the whale would by all hands be considered a noble dish were there not so much of him; but when you come to sit down before a meat pie nearly 100 feet long, it takes away your appetite.

***Herman Melville** (1819-1891), American novelist and poet. One-time professional whale hunter. From 'Moby Dick' (published 1851)*

*Professor Branestawm's Pancake Machine:*

'Here are the flour bin, the egg receptacle, the milk churn, and the sugar canister and the lemon squisher This is the pancake pan, and this is the thickening regulator, by means of which you can have pancakes any thickness you like. Here is the centrifugal tossing gear with adjustable self-changing height regulator, and my own patent device for calculating the number of tosses required for pancakes of different thicknesses.'

'Will it go wrong?'

'Certainly not.'

***Norman Hunter** (1899-1995), children's author, stage magician. 34 books*

***Heath Robinson** (1872-1944), artist, illustrator and cartoonist*

*From 'The Incredible Adventures of Professor Branestawm' published 1933.*

*Coca-Cola logos:*

Coca-Cola was registered as a trademark in 1887, and since then it has become one of the most recognised images on Earth. Below are some of the Coca-Cola logos employed in different locations around the world:

Enjoy
Coca-Cola

Enjoy
コカ・コーラ

Japan

请喝
可口可乐

China

ดื่ม
โคคา-โคลา

Thailand

마시자
코카·콜라

Korea

اشرب
كوكا كولا

Morocco

Уживајте во
Кока-Кола

Russia

可口可乐

China (again)

שתו
קוקה-קולה

Israel

*Catchphrases that are good enough to eat:*

It's all done in the best possible taste – ***Kenny Everett***

Beulah, peel me a grape – ***Mae West** in 'I'm no Angel'*

Dig for victory – *wartime slogan from **Sir Reginald Dorman-Smith***

He can't fart and chew gum at the same time – ***President Lyndon Johnson's** description of President Gerald Ford*

Here's a pretty kettle of fish – ***Queen Mary,** referring to the abdication crisis of 1936*

If you can't stand the heat, get out of the kitchen – ***President Harry Truman,** on his decision not to stand for election in 1952*

No such thing as a free lunch – *19th century saying immortalised by Milton Friedman in the title of his book*

Pass the sick-bag, Alice – *used by **John Junor** in his Sunday Express column*

Pile it high, sell it cheap – ***Sir John Cohen,** founder of Tesco*

Probably the best lager in the world – *Carlsberg advertisement, unforgettably voiced by Orson Welles*

The thinking-man's crumpet – *coined by **Frank Muir** to describe broadcaster Joan Bakewell*

- To carry the same amount of food, air freight burns 50 litres of fuel, a ship burns one litre, and road transport six litres.
- Distributing food by plane around the world releases 50 times more $CO_2$ than if it went by sea.
- 1kg of asparagus flown from California produces 4kg of carbon dioxide. If it were grown in Europe, 900 times less energy would be produced.
- The price of sending by sea fell over 70% between 1980 and 2000.
- In 2001, for every 1,000 fruit products bought in the UK, only six were grown in the UK.

- One tonne of food in the UK now travels an average of 123km (76 miles) before it reaches the shelves, compared with 82km (51 miles) in 1978.
- More than one third of lorry traffic on UK roads is carrying food.

- If your Sunday lunch consists of beef from Australia, runner beans from Thailand, potatoes from Italy, carrots from South Africa, broccoli from Guatemala and fruit from America and New Zealand, the ingredients could have travelled a total of 490,000 miles. All of these ingredients are grown in Britain.

*Helpful advice found on food packaging:*

- *On a bag of Fritos:* You could be a winner! No purchase necessary. Details inside.
- *On Swanson Frozen Dinners:* Serving suggestion: Defrost.
- *On Tesco's tiramisu dessert (printed on bottom):* Do not turn upside down.
- *On Marks & Spencer Bread Pudding:* Product will be hot after heating.
- *On Sainsbury's peanuts:* Warning: Contains nuts.
- *On an American Airlines packet of nuts:* Instructions: Open packet. Eat nuts.
- *On a Japanese food processor:* Not to be used for the other use.

'Hold hard a minute, then!' said the Rat. He looped the painter through a ring in his landing stage, climbed up into his hole above, and... reappeared staggering under a fat, wicker luncheon basket.

'Shove that under your feet,' he observed to the Mole, as he passed it down into the boat. Then he untied the painter and took the sculls again.

'What's inside it?' asked the Mole, wriggling with curiosity.

'There's cold chicken inside it,' replied the Rat briefly; 'coldtonguecold hamcoldbeefpickledgherkinssaladfrenchrollscressandwidgepottedmeatging erbeerlemonadesodawater...'

'O stop, stop,' cried the Mole in ecstasies: 'This is too much!'

***Kenneth Grahame** (1859-1932), writer, particularly for children. Secretary of Bank of England. From 'Wind in the Willows' published 1908*

God of goodness, bless our food,
Keep us in a pleasant mood.
Bless the cook and all who serve us,
From indigestion, Lord preserve us.
Amen

They drink whisky to keep them warm, then they put ice in it to make it cool; then they put some sugar in it to make it sweet and then they put a slice of lemon in it to make it sour. Then they say, 'Here's to you' and drink it themselves.

***BN Chakravarty** (1904-1976), Indian Ambassador to Netherlands, High Commissioner to United Kingdom and Canada. Educated Scottish Church College in Calcutta, University College London and School of Oriental Studies. Chemist. District judge*

In a corner of the kitchen they found bottles bearing the labels of various mineral waters – Evian, Vichy, Malvern – all empty. It was Mr Youkoumian's practice to replenish them from the foetid well at the back of the house.

***Evelyn Waugh** (1903-1966), novelist, biographer, journalist. Served in Royal Marines and Royal Horse Guards. From 'Black Mischief', published 1932*

While he forth from the closet brought a heap
Of candied apple, quince, and plum, and gourd
With jellies soother than the creamy curd,
And lucent syrops, tinct with cinnamon;
Manna and dates, in argosy transferr'd
From Fez; and spiced dainties, every one,
From silken Samarcand to cedar'd Lebanon.

*John Keats (1795-1821),*
*from 'The Eve of St Agnes', 1820*

Every times I lose weight it finds me again.

*Written on the lavatory wall in a Brixton pub*

A fat brown goose lay at one end of the table and at the other end, on a bed of creased paper strewn with sprigs of parsley, lay a great ham, stripped of its outer skin and peppered over with crust crumbs, a neat paper frill round its shin and beside this was a round of spiced beef. Between these rival ends ran parallel lines of side-dishes: two little minsters of jelly, red and yellow; a shallow dish full of blocks of blancmange and red jam, a large green leaf-shaped dish with a stalk-shaped handle on which lay bunches of purple raisins and peeled almonds, a companion dish on which lay a solid rectangle of Smyrna figs, a dish of custard topped with grated nutmeg, a small bowl full of chocolates and sweets wrapped in gold and silver papers and a glass vase in which stood some tall celery stalks. In the centre of the table there stood, as sentries to a fruit-stand which upheld a pyramid of oranges and American apples, two squat old-fashioned decanters of cut glass, one containing port and the other dark sherry. On the closed square piano a pudding in a huge yellow dish law in waiting...

***James Augustine Aloysius Joyce** (1882-1941), Irish novelist, poet critic. Adult life in Zurich, Paris and Trieste. From 'The Dead', 1914*

# 11 | Legal

Question to lawyer:
'If I give you £500, will you answer two questions?'
'Certainly. What's the second question?'

Sir, The call of Robert Rhodes, QC for judges' retirement age to be raised to 80 is likely to fall on deaf ears.
Lamb Chambers, London EC4

*The Times*

*The first barrister reputed to have earned £1 million was* ***Sir Desmond de Silva*** *(1939-2018). A Sri Lankan called to the bar in 1964 he married Princess Katarina of Yugoslavia. Privy Councillor. Inherited the island of Taprobane off Sri Lanka. United Nations Chief War Crimes prosecutor in Sierra Leone to where he had foie gras flown out from France.*

The experiences both of Counsel and Judge are spent sorting out the difficulties of people who, upon the recommendation of people they did not know, signed documents which they did not read, to buy goods they did not need, with money they had not got.

***Gilbert Harding*** *(1907-1960), journalist and TV personality.*
*'The rudest man in Britain'*

Compromise is the best and cheapest lawyer.

***Robert Louis Stevenson*** *(1850-1894), novelist and travel writer.*
*Family designed lighthouses. Died at his home in Samoa*

A good lawyer knows the law; a clever one takes the judge to lunch.

*Mark Twain (born Samuel Clemens) (1835-1910),*
*American writer, humourist. Ship's pilot*

The nine points of law are said to be:

1. A good deal of money;
2. A good deal of patience;
3. A good cause;
4. A good lawyer;
5. A good counsel;
6. Good witnesses:
7. A good jury;
8. A good judge;
9. Good luck.

In the old days all you needed was a handshake. Nowadays you need forty lawyers.

*Jimmy Hoffa (1913-1975) (disappeared), American*
*President of Teamsters Union. Jailed for fraud*

A Dutch court rejected a claim that Pastafarianism is a religion and so denied Mienke de Wilde, a follower of the Church of the Flying Spaghetti Monster, the right to wear a colander on her head in her passport and driving licence photographs.

***David Pannick, QC, Baron Pannick** (b 1956), barrister, Fellow of All Souls. From 'Review of Audacious Advocacy',*

No brilliance is needed in the law. Nothing but common sense, and relatively clean fingernails.

***John Mortimer** (1923-2009), barrister, dramatist and author*

Lawyers enjoy a little mystery, you know. Why, if everybody came forward and told the truth, the whole truth, and nothing but the truth straight out, we should all retire to the workhouse.

***Dorothy L Sayers** (1893-1957), scholar, crime writer, poet and playwright. First class degree in modern languages at Oxford*

If a man's word is as good as his bond, always take his bond.

*Advice to lawyers*

A judge asked counsel, who had mentioned the London Coliseum, where it was, adding that he thought it was the place where Romans threw Christians to the lions. 'My Lord,' explained counsel, 'it is ten minutes' walk from the Trocadero, where the Lyons throw food to the Christians'.

# 12 | Advice

Nothing makes you look older
than attempting to look young.

***Karl Lagerfeld** (1933-2019),*
*German fashion designer of Chanel*

Age is opportunity no less,
Than youth itself, though in another dress,
And as the evening twilight fades away,
The sky is filled with stars, invisible by day…

***Henry Longfellow** (1807-1882), American poet. Translated Horace and works in Spanish, French and Italian*

Be kind to unkind people. They need it the most.

***Ashleigh Brilliant** (b 1933), cartoonist and epigrammist*

Kindness is the touch of an angel's hand.

***James Gordon** (1917-1967), Filipino mayor of Olangapo. Developer of orphanages*

Nothing is ever lost by courtesy. It is the cheapest of pleasures, costs nothing, and conveys much.

***Erastus Wiman** (1834-1904), Canadian journalist and businessman. Developed Staten Island, NY*

# Manners makyth man

*Motto of Winchester College, founded in 1382 by William of Wykeham (1324-1404), Bishop of Winchester. Also founder of New College, Oxford. Lord Chancellor*

Why be disagreeable, when with a little effort you can be impossible?

***Douglas Woodruff** (1897-1978), US federal judge*

I believe that the rendering of useful service is the common duty of mankind and that only in the purifying fire of sacrifice is the dross of selfishness consumed and the greatness of the human soul set free.

***John Rockefeller Jr** (1874-1960), American financier and philanthropist. Son of John Rockefeller of Standard Oil and father of five famous Rockefellers*

Mingle a little folly with your wisdom; a little nonsense now and then is pleasant.

***Horatio Flaccus** (known as **Horace**) (65-8 BC), poet, soldier, biographer*

Just be yourself, there is no one better.

*Taylor Swift (b 1989), American singer-songwriter. 50 million albums sold*

The world is disgracefully managed, one does not know to whom to complain.

***Ronald Firbank** (1886-1926), novelist. Gay, cannabis consumer*

In matters of style, swim with the current; in matters of principle, stand like a rock.

***Thomas Jefferson** (1743-1826), American statesman, diplomat, lawyer, architect. Founding Father and 3rd President of United States*

Buy on the rumour, sell on the news.

*Wall Street adage*

Buy when there's blood on the streets.

***Baron Guy de Rothschild** (1909-2007), French banker and owner of Rothschild Frères. Racehorse breeder and art collector*

It is a diarist's job hazard that some stories will have been around the block a few times. Occasionally, a reader may email to say he first heard a joke in 1822. I now have a way to pre-empt these complaints thanks to a letter in The Spectator. Quentin Crisp used to begin anecdotes by telling his audience: 'Don't stop me if I've told you this before; I'd like to hear it again myself'.

***Patrick Kidd***

Beware that you do not lose the substance by grasping at the shadow.

***Aesop** (620-564 BC), Greek fabulist*

Do not follow where the path may lead. Go instead where there is no path and leave a trail.

***Harold R McAlindon.***
*From 'The Little Book of Big Ideas'. Published 1999*

Let us try to see things as they are, and not wish to be wiser than God.

***Gustave Flaubert** (1821-1880), French novelist*

You seldom improve quality by cutting costs, but you can often cut costs by improving quality.

***Karl Albrecht** (1920-2014), German founder of Aldi supermarket chain. Reclusive. Germany's richest man*

The best form of flattery is to master the art of listening.

*Chinese proverb*

A nickel will get you on the subway, but garlic will get you a seat.

*New York Jewish saying*

Never wrestle with a strong man nor bring a rich man to court.

*Latin proverb*

When buffalo battle in the marsh, it's the frogs who pay.

*Greek proverb*

In any moment of decision, the best thing you can do is the right thing, the next best thing is the wrong thing, and the worst thing you can do is nothing.

***Theodore Roosevelt** (1858-1919), 26th President of United States. Naturalist and conservationist*

It's the good girls who keep diaries. The bad girls never have the time.

***Tallulah Bankhead** (1902-1968), American actress and wit. Married seven times. Prodigious memory. 300 acting roles.*

Education is what you get when you read the fine print; experience is what you get when you don't.

*'Pete' Seeger (1919-2014), American folk singer and anti-war activist. 19 music awards*

The hardest thing to learn in life is which bridge to cross and which to burn.

***David Russell** (b 1958), American film director and screenwriter. 12 Academy Awards and Nominations*

The Ten Commandments should be treated like an examination. Only six need to be attempted.

***Bertrand Russell, 3rd Earl Russell** (1872-1970), philosopher, historian, mathematician, pacifist. Nobel Laureate for Literature. 157 published works and 18 volumes of unpublished work*

A true friend is someone who is there for you when he'd rather be anywhere else.

***Leonard Wein** (1948-2017), American comic book writer. Originator of Captain Marvel and Batman*

Lead us not into temptation. Just tell us where it is; we'll find it.

***Sam Levenson** (1911-1980), American humourist and writer*

Do not worry about avoiding temptation. As you grow older it will avoid you.

***Joey Adams** (b 1968), American actress and film director. 40 films*

Instant gratification takes too long.

***Carrie Fisher** (1956-2016), American actress, writer and comedienne. Daughter of Eddie Fisher and Debbie Reynolds*

*Letter from an executed Yugoslav partisan to his unborn child in World War II:*

My child,
In the life ahead of you, keep your capacity for faith and belief, but let your judgment watch what you believe. Keep your love of life, but throw away your fear of death. Life must be loved or it is lost, but it should never be loved too well. Keep your wonder at great and noble things, like sunlight and thunder, the rain and the stars, and the greatness of heroes. Keep your heart hungry for new knowledge. Keep your hatred of a lie, and keep your power of indignation ... I am ashamed to leave you an uncomfortable world, but someday it will be better. And when that day comes, you will thank God for the greatest blessing man can conceive, living in peace.

Treasure the people, then the land, and the ruler last of all.

***Mengzi** (Meng Ke) (372-289 BC), Chinese Confucian philosopher*

# 13 | Politics, the Press, Journalism, Economics and the Military

Jacob Rees-Mogg (b 1969), MP and Leader of House of Commons and dubbed 'Honourable Member for 18th Century', played the stock market aged 11. At the same age, he went to Annual General Meetings invariably voting against the accounts on the grounds that the dividend was too low. He had four bank accounts. On opening his first at Lloyds, the manager asked him why he had chosen that bank. Jacob (known as Jakit) replied that he liked their picture of a horse and that they paid a half a per cent more interest than others.

*The Albany column of Kenneth Rose (1924-2014) in the Sunday Telegraph ran for 36 years. He described it as* 'erudite, gently snobbish, appealing to minority tastes such as clavichords, Zanzibar liqueurs, pelota or Siamese orders of chivalry'. *He wanted it to be about* 'people who matter, except for sportsmen or those famous for being famous'. *Rose knew most of 'those who matter' and was known by The Telegraph as* 'The secretary-general of the Establishment'. *Others knew him as Climbing Rose in view of his acquaintance with the highest levels of society. His journals were left to the Bodleian Library and filled 400 boxes.*

*Here are a few gossipy nuggets from 'Who's In, Who's Out?' and 'Who Loses, Who Wins?' Volumes I and II of the journals of Kenneth Rose, edited by Richard Thorne. Published 2018 and 2020:*

- Harold Macmillan turned down the Order of the Garter with the comment 'One cannot join every club one is asked to'.

- King George V came to stay at Chatsworth and said that he would like to present Spencer Devonshire, 8th Duke of Devonshire, with a GCVO before dinner. The Duke churlishly said 'I hope it doesn't interfere with my dressing for dinner'. It did. He came down to dinner ten minutes late with the GCVO star upside down and his fly buttons undone.

- Winston Churchill was having lunch with Somerset Maugham when Lord Cork and Orrey was mentioned. Winston remarks 'He talks too much. When Lord Cork has finished, Lord Orrey starts'.

*Admiral William Boyle, 12th Earl of Cork and Orrey (1872-1967), C-in-C Home Fleet 1938*

- King Farouk of Egypt (1920-1965), failed his entry exams for the Royal Military Academy, Woolwich, complaining that in Egypt he was always given the answers. (He had previously failed the entrance exam for Eton for the same reason).

- When Rose was staying at Balmoral, Princess Helena Victoria (1870-1948, granddaughter of Queen Victoria) told the story of an old profligate who had gone to live in Ireland. He died and his son sends a telegram back to relations in England: 'Father gone, safe in the arms of Jesus'. Unfortunately the telegram was garbled and the son received the reply 'Where has he gone and who is Jessie?'.

- Sir Edward Heath (Prime Minister 1970-1974 and noted musician) was conducting a charity concert when a telephone rang during the Siegfried Idyll. Rose's neighbour whispered to him 'It's Wagner calling to complain'.

- Louise Mountbatten when later Queen of Sweden, 1950-1965, was visiting Uppsala Cathedral. The Archbishop courteously spoke English to her – but imperfectly. On a tour of the Cathedral's treasures, he approached a chest of drawers. 'With your permission, your Highness, I will now open these trousers and reveal the treasures inside'.

- Leonid Brezhnev (1906-1982) was showing his mother his splendid flat in Moscow, his magnificent apartment in the Kremlin, his luxurious dacha and his palatial residence in the Crimea. His mother admired them all but added 'Be careful, my son. If those Communists hear about all this, they will take it away from you'.

---

You go to Boodles for good food, you go to the Carlton to talk politics and you go to White's to be insulted.

*__Harold Macmillan__ (1894-1986), Prime Minister, known as 'Super Mac'. Member of many clubs*

At times like these, it's good to recall the graceful and reflective words of Dick Tuck's concession speech when he lost a California Senate race in 1966: 'The people have spoken, the bastards'.

*__Dick Tuck__ (1924-2018), American political consultant. Remark following loss of 1966 California State Senate selection*

Mr Speaker, I withdraw my statement that half the cabinet are asses – half the cabinet are not asses.

*__Benjamin Disraeli,__ 1st Earl of Beaconsfield (1804-1881). Twice Conservative Prime Minister. Classicist*

President Roosevelt proved that a President could serve for life; President Truman proved that anyone could be President; President Eisenhower proved that your country can be run without a president.

*__Nikita Krushschev__ (1894-1971), Soviet premier. Metal worker, commissar of construction battalion*

*Presidential coincidences:*

- Lincoln was elected President in 1860. Kennedy was elected President in 1960.
- Both were assassinated in the presence of their wives, shot in the head from behind. Booth shot Lincoln in a theatre and ran to a warehouse. Oswald shot Kennedy from a warehouse and ran to a theatre.
- John Wilkes Booth was born in 1839. Lee Harvey Oswald was born in 1939.
- Both assassins were killed before their trial.
- Lincoln's secretary was named Kennedy. Kennedy's secretary was named Lincoln.

I want the whole of Europe to have one currency; it will make trading much easier.

*Letter from __Napoleon Bonaparte__ (born Napoleone di Buonaparte) (1769-1821), to his brother Louis in May 1807*

The Tories' main problem is that they don't have anyone you'd want to go to bed with.

*__Anne Robinson__ (b 1944), journalist, alcoholic and controversial TV presenter*

He is forever poised between a cliché and an indiscretion.

*Malcolm Muggeridge* (1903-1990), *journalist and satirist. Russian correspondent for Manchester Guardian. Converted to Christianity. About Sir Anthony Eden (1897-1977), Conservative Prime Minister*

Britain has invented a new missile. It's called the civil servant – it doesn't work and it can't be fired.

***Sir Walter Walker*** *(1912-2001), General, Commander-in-Chief Northern Europe 1969-1972. DSO and bar*

Never stand between a dog and a lamp post.

***Stanley Baldwin,*** *1st Earl of Bewdley (1867-1947), three times Conservative Prime Minister. Third class degree at Cambridge*

I would rather be an opportunist and float, than go to the bottom with my principles around my neck.

*Ibid*

A man who could start a fight in an empty room.

*Of Sir Gerald Kaufman (1930-2017), forthright Labour politician*

I don't want the truth. I want something I can tell Parliament.

*Prime Minister Jim Hacker in TV series 'Yes Prime Minister'*

The budget should be balanced, the Treasury should be refilled, public debt should be reduced, the arrogance of officialdom should be tempered and controlled, and the assistance to foreign lands should be curtailed lest Rome become bankrupt. People must again learn to work, instead of living on public assistance.

***Marcus Tullius Cicero** (106-43 BC), Roman statesman, lawyer, philosopher. Fluent Greek*

Politicians and diapers have one thing in common. They should both be changed regularly, and for the same reasons.

***Jose Maria de Eça de Queirós** (1845-1900), Portuguese writer and diplomat*

Politicians can forgive almost anything in the way of abuse; they can forgive subversion, revolution, being contradicted, exposed as liars, even ridiculed, but they can never forgive being ignored.

***Auberon Waugh** (1939-2001), journalist and novelist*

The cardinal rule of politics: never get caught in bed with a dead girl or a live boy.

***Edwin Edwards** (b 1927), American politician. Served four terms as Governor of Louisiana. Imprisoned for racketeering*

In politics one should not commit suicide as one might live to regret it.

***Winston Churchill** (1874-1965), British Prime Minister 1940-1945*

I have often had to eat my words, and I must confess that I have always found it a wholesome diet.

*Ibid*

When the eagles are silent, the parrots begin to jabber.

*Ibid*

Man does not live by words alone, despite the fact that he sometimes has to eat them.

***Adlai Stevenson*** *(1845-1914), US Vice President.*
*Artificial jaw from cigar-induced cancer*

Economic forecasts are like sausages; when you've seen how they are made you don't want to go near them.

***Matthew Goodwin*** *(b 1981), Professor of Politics*

I have often regretted my speech, never my silence.

***Publilius Syrus*** *(85-43 BC), Syrian brought to Rome as a slave. Writer*

It has been my experience that folks who have no vices have very few virtues.

***Abraham Lincoln*** *(1809-1865), lawyer and 16th President of United States. Led country through Civil War. Abolished slavery*

***Willie Hamilton*** *(1917-2000), Scottish Member of Parliament, harangued Prime Minister Wilson on the issue of Britain's membership of the Common Market.* 'First we're in, then we're out – it's like coitus interruptus'. *The House of Commons was stunned into silence but then erupted into laughter when a member cried* 'Withdraw!'

'Do you have any skeletons in your cupboard?'
'Dear boy, I can hardly close the door.'

*Alan Clark (1928-1999), flamboyant right-wing politician, diarist, barrister, military historian*

If it were not for the government, we would have nothing to laugh at.

*Sébastien-Roch Nicolas (known as Nicolas Chamfort) (1741-1794), French writer and member of Académie Française*

Capitalism is the exploitation of man by man. Communism is the other way round.

*Sir Rodric Braithwaite (b 1932), diplomat and author*

Diplomacy is the art of letting someone else have your way.

***Sir David Frost** (1939-2013), journalist, television personality and comedian. Interviewed eight British Prime Ministers and seven American Presidents*

Diplomacy is the process by which people choose the man who'll get the blame

***Bertrand Russell, 3rd Earl Russell** (1872-1970), philosopher, polymath, mathematician, historian, writer, social activist and pacifist. Philanderer. Zionist. Nobel Prize for Literature*

A diplomat is a man who always remembers a woman's birthday but never remembers her age.

***Robert Frost** (1874-1963), American poet*

Diplomacy is to do and say the nastiest things in the nicest way.

***Isaac Goldberg** (1887-1938), American journalist, biographer. Critic. Fluent in seven languages*

Diplomacy: a continuation of war by other means.
*[A play on the maxim of Clausewitz: 'War is the continuation of politics by other means']*

***Zhou Enlai** (1898-1976). 1st Premier of the Peoples' Republic of China*

Diplomacy is about surviving until the next century; politics is about surviving until Friday afternoon.

*Sir Humphrey Appleby on the TV show 'Yes Prime Minister'*

Diplomacy is the art of saying things in such a way that nobody can be sure what you mean.

*'Diplomacy: Lying in State'*

There are few ironclad rules of diplomacy, but to one there is no exception. When an official reports that talks were useful, it can safely be concluded that nothing was accomplished.

***John 'Ken' Galbraith** (1908-2006), Canadian/American economist and diplomat. 6'5" tall. Medal of Freedom twice. Légion d'honneur*

The duty of a patriot is to protect his country from its government.

***Thomas Paine** (1737-1809), American politician and revolutionary*

I think that people want peace so much that one of these days governments had better get out of their way and let them have it.

***Dwight 'Ike' Eisenhower** (1890-1969), American army general and 34th President of the United States. In letter of 1950 to Prime Minister Harold Macmillan*

You can build a throne with bayonets, but you can't sit on it for long.

***Boris Yeltsin** (1931-2007), President of Russia 1991-1999. Civil engineer and orthodox Christian*

The most radical revolutionary will become a conservative on the day after the revolution.

***Joanna (Hannah) Arendt** (1906-1975), German/American political theorist and Jewish activist*

All tip and no iceberg.

*Paul Keating (b 1944), Prime Minister of Australia. About a political opponent*

Prime ministers are wedded to the truth, but like many other married couples they sometimes live apart.

*HH Munro, 'Saki' (1870-1916), short story writer and satirist*

In America, anyone can become president. That's the problem.

*George Carlin (1937-2008), American actor, author and comedian*

The Sovereign under constitutional monarchy has three rights:

The right to be consulted;
The right to encourage;
The right to warn.

A monarch of great sense and sagacity would want no others.

*Walter Bagehot (1826-1877), journalist, businessman, lawyer*

*Economic models explained:*

***A French Corporation*** – You have two cows. You go on strike, organise a riot, and block the roads, because you want three cows.

***A Japanese Corporation*** – You have two cows. You redesign them so they are one-tenth the size of an ordinary cow and produce 20 times the milk.

***A German Corporation*** – You have two cows. You re-engineer them so they live for 100 years, eat once a month, and milk themselves.

***An Italian Corporation*** – You have two cows, but you don't know where they are. You decide to have lunch.

*A Russian Corporation* – You have two cows. You count them and learn you have five cows. You count them again and learn you have 42 cows. You count them again and learn you have two cows. You stop counting cows and open another bottle of vodka.

*A Swiss Corporation* – You have 5,000 cows. None of them belong to you. You charge the owners for storing them.

*A Chinese Corporation* – You have two cows. You have 300 people milking them. You claim that you have full employment, and high bovine productivity. You arrest the newsman who reported anything different.

*An Indian Corporation* – You have two cows. You worship them.

*A British Corporation* – You have two cows. Both are mad.

*An Australian Corporation* – You have two cows. Business seems pretty good. You close the office and go for a few beers to celebrate.

A *New Zealand Corporation* – You have two cows. The one on the left looks very attractive.

*An American Corporation* – You have two cows. You sell one, and force the other to produce the milk of four cows. Later, you hire a consultant to analyse why the cow has dropped dead.

***Communism*** – You have two cows. The State takes both and gives you some milk.

***Socialism*** – You have two cows. You give one to your neighbour.

***Fascism*** – You have two cows. The State takes both and sells you some milk.

***Nazism*** – You have two cows. The State takes both and shoots you.

***Bureaucratism*** – You have two cows. The State takes both, shoots one, milks the other, and then throws away the milk.

***Capitalism*** – You have two cows. You sell one and buy a bull.

***Enron*** – You have two cows and sell three of them to your publicly listed company using letters of credit arranged by your brother-in-law. You transfer the milking rights of what you claim are six cows to a Cayman Island Co secretly owned by a majority shareholder and sell rights to seven cows back to Enron. The annual report says that the company owns eight cows.

If we want things to stay as they are, things will have to change.

***Giuseppe di Lampedusa*** *(1896-1957), Sicilian novelist. Author of 'The Leopard'*

Having a little inflation is like being a little bit pregnant.

***Leon Henderson*** *(1895-1986), American economist*

If I'd known how wonderful grandchildren were going to be,
I would've had them first.

***Joanna Trollope*** *(b 1943), novelist. Scholarship to Oxford University*

All God's children are not beautiful. Most of God's children are, in fact, barely presentable.

***Frances 'Fran' Lebowitz*** *(b 1950), American author and wit. Famously resistant to technology*

I believe in an open mind, but not so open that your brains fall out.

***Arthur Ochs Sulzberger Jr*** *(b 1951), American publisher of The New York Times*

*William Gladstone:* 'Mr Disraeli, you will probably die by the hangman's noose or from a vile disease.'
*Benjamin Disraeli:* 'Sir, that depends on whether I embrace your principles or your mistress.'

We talked of different forms of government; and it was remarked what difficulties an excess of liberalism presents, as it calls forth the demands of individuals, and, from the quantity of wishes, raises uncertainty as to which should be satisfied. In the long run, over-great goodness, mildness, and moral delicacy will not do, while underneath there is a mixed and sometimes vicious world to manage and hold in respect.

***Johann von Goethe*** *(1749-1832), German writer of poetry and novels, scientist, statesman and lawyer. From 'Conversations with Goethe' by Johann Eckermann*

Lloyd George was born a cad and never forgot it. Winston was born a gentleman and never remembered it.

***Stanley Baldwin, 1st Earl Baldwin of Bewdley*** *(1867-1947), between the world wars. Prime Minister on three occasions*

## IN MEMORIAM

UK Democracy on 29th March 2019, aged 312. It was with sad regret that Democracy died quietly in her sleep at 11pm, on the 29th March 2019. The cause of death was by foul play and the culprits have yet to be brought to justice. Democracy campaigned for the rule of law, human rights and free elections. She listened to everyone and favoured the majority in all her decisions. She will be sorely missed. God have mercy on her soul.

The best government is a benevolent tyranny tempered by an occasional assassination.

***François-Marie Arouet (known as Voltaire)** (1694-1778),*
*French writer, historian and philosopher.*
*Author of 2,000 books and pamphlets*

If Gladstone fell into the Thames, that would be a misfortune, and if anybody pulled him out that, I suppose, would be a calamity.

***Benjamin Disraeli, 1st Earl of Beaconsfield** (1804-1881),*
*Jewish politician and twice Prime Minister. Political opponent of liberal William Gladstone*

A government is the only known vessel that leaks from the top.

***Dean Acheson** (1893-1971), American lawyer, statesman and diplomat*

In Britain, to govern is difficult. In Italy it is pointless.

*Senior Italian official, quoted by William Hague*
*in The Daily Telegraph*

The Right Hon. was a tubby little chap who looked as if he had been poured into his clothes and had forgotten to say 'When!'

*Misnomers:*

The Holy Roman Empire: 'Neither Holy, Roman nor an Empire'

***Francois-Marie Arouet**, known as **Voltaire** (1694-1778).*
*French writer, historian and philosopher.*
*Wrote 20,000 letters. Exciled to Britain.*

The Lord Privy Seal: 'Neither a lord, nor a privy nor a seal'

***Sydney Bailey**. From 'The Future of the House of Lords',*
*Hansard Society*

---

Think where man's glory most begins and ends
And say my glory was 'I had such friends'

***William Butler Yeats** (1865-1939), Irish poet and politician.*
*Dedication to Michael and Edna Longley, Irish poets*

Being Prime Minister is the easiest job in the world. Everyone else has an instrument. You just stand there and conduct.

***James 'Jim' Callaghan, Baron Callaghan** (1912-2005), Prime Minister 1976-1979. Only politician to have held all four Great Offices of State. Naval officer*

Politicians in Malaysia were criticised during a recent general election for promising a place in Heaven. The Electoral Commission took a dim view saying that this could be disadvantageous to other candidates.

The best reason for going into politics is to stop people bossing you around and taking your money for no good reason.

***Boris Johnson** (b 1964), politician, writer, Prime Minister from 2019. Mayor of London 2007-2016*

Never believe anything in politics until it has been officially denied.

***Otto Leopold** (known as Otto von Bismarck) (1815-1898), German Chancellor 1867-1871. Unified German states*

The word politics is derived from two words – poly, meaning many, and tics, meaning small blood-sucking insects.

Politics consists of choosing between the disastrous and the unpalatable.

***JK Galbraith** (1908-2006), Canadian economist and diplomat. Became American citizen. Professor at Harvard, Berkeley and Cambridge*

A politician is an animal that can sit on a fence and yet keep both ears to the ground.

***Henry Mencken** (1880-1956), American journalist, satirist and scholar*

Loyalty is a fine thing but in excess it fills political graveyards.

***Neil Kinnock, Baron Kinnock** (b 1942), Welsh politician and leader of Labour Party 1983-1992*

After Funland in Leicester Square and the arrival lounge at Rome airport, it is said that the central library of the House of Commons is the third easiest in Europe to pick up people.

***Alan Clark** (1928-1999), author, diarist. Flamboyant Member of Parliament, barrister*

I am more or less happy when being praised, not very comfortable when being abused but I have moments of uneasiness when being explained.

***Arthur Balfour, 1st Earl Balfour** (1848-1930), Prime Minister 1902-1905. Originator of The Balfour Declaration in Palestine*

There are two problems in my life. The political ones are insoluble and the economic ones are incomprehensible.

***Sir Alec Douglas-Home, Baron Home** (1903-1995), Prime Minister 1963-1964. Disclaimed peerage*

No woman in my time will be Prime Minister or Chancellor or Foreign Secretary – not the top jobs. Anyway I wouldn't want to be Prime Minister.

***Margaret Thatcher, Baroness Thatcher*** *(1925-2013), research chemist, barrister, first woman Prime Minister 1979-1990*

I am extraordinarily patient, provided I get my own way.

*Ibid*

PROCLAIM LIBERTY THROUGHOUT ALL THE LAND UNTO ALL THE INHABITANTS THEREOF

*Inscription on the Liberty Bell in Philadelphia. From Leviticus XXV,10*

*Military:*

Soldiers, what I have to offer you is fatigue, danger, struggle and death; the chill of the cold night in the free air, and heat under the burning sun; no lodgings, no munitions, no provisions, but forced marches, dangerous watchposts, and the continual struggle with the bayonet against batteries. Those who love freedom and their country may follow me.

***Giuseppe Garibaldi*** *(1807-1882), Italian general, patriot and dedicated republican. Commander in Uruguayan Civil War and Franco-Prussian War*

We shall not fail or falter; we shall not weaken or tire. Neither the sudden shock of battle, nor the long-drawn trials of vigilance and exertion will wear us down. Give us the tools and we will finish the job.

*National radio broadcast, 9th February 1941 by* ***Winston Churchill***

To be prepared for war is the most effective means of preserving peace.

*George Washington (1732-1799), American statesman, general and 1st President of United States*

Older men declare war.
But it is youth that must fight and die.

*Herbert Hoover (1874-1964), American engineer, 31st President of United States*

A leader is a man who has the ability to get other people to do what they don't want to do, and like it.

*Harry Truman (1884-1972), 33rd President of United States. Musician and army officer*

Leadership consists of nothing but taking responsibility for everything that goes wrong and giving your subordinates credit for everything that goes well.

*Dwight 'Ike' Eisenhower (1890-1969), American general, statesman. 34th President of the United States*

*World War II US army maxims:*

If it moves, salute it.
If it doesn't move, pick it up.
If you can't pick it up, paint it.

Keep your mouth shut, your bowels open and never volunteer.

Shape up or ship out.

## 21 ARMY GROUP

## PERSONAL MESSAGE FROM THE C-IN-C.
## TO BE READ OUT TO ALL TROOPS:

1. The time has come to deal the enemy a terrific blow in Western Europe. The blow will be struck by the combined sea, land, and air forces of the Allies - together constituting one great Allied team, under the supreme command of General Eisenhower.

2. On the eve of this great adventure I send my best wishes to every soldier in the Allied team. To us is given the honour of striking a blow for freedom which will live in history; and in the better days that lie ahead men will speak with pride of our doings. We have a great and righteous cause. Let us pray that 'The Lord Mighty in Battle' will go forth with our armies, and that His special providence will aid us in the struggle.

3. I want every soldier to know that I have complete confidence in the successful outcome of the operations that we are now about to begin.With stout hearts, and with enthusiasm for the contest, let us go forward to victory.

4. And, as we enter the battle, let us recall the words of a famous soldier [the Marquess of Montrose, 1612-1650] spoken many years ago:

   He either fears his fate too much,
   Or his desserts are small,
   Who dare not put it to the touch,
   To win or lose it all.

5. Good luck to each one of you. And good hunting on the mainland of Europe.

B.L. Montgomery
General
C-in-C 21 Army Group

1944

*Bernard Montgomery (1887-1976), 1st Viscount of Alamein.*
*Field Marshal. General in First and Second World Wars*

## INSTRUMENT OF SURRENDER
## OF ALL GERMAN ARMED FORCES,
## IN HOLLAND, IN NORTHWEST GERMANY INCLUDING
## ALL ISLANDS, AND IN DENMARK

1. The German Command agrees to the surrender of all German armed forces in Holland, in northwest Germany including the Frisian Islands, and Heligoland and all other islands, in Schleswig-Holstein, and in Denmark, to the C-in-C 21 Army Group. This to include all naval ships in these areas. These forces to lay down their arms and to surrender unconditionally.

2. All hostilities on land, on sea, or in the air by German forces in the above areas to cease at 0800 hrs British Double Summer Time on Saturday 5th May 1945.

3. The German Command to carry out at once, and without argument or comment, all further orders that will be issued by the Allied Powers on any subject.

4. Disobedience of orders, or failure to comply with them, will be regarded as a breach of these surrender terms and will be dealt with by the Allied Powers in accordance with the accepted laws and usages of war.

5. This instrument of surrender is independent of, without prejudice to, and will be superseded by any general instrument of surrender imposed by or on behalf of the Allied Powers and applicable to Germany and the German armed forces as a whole.

6. This instrument of surrender is written in English and German. The English version is the authentic text.

7. The decision of the Allied Powers will be final if any doubt or dispute arises as to the meaning or interpretation of the surrender terms.

B.L. Montgomery
Field-Marshal
C-in-C 21 Army Group

4 May 1945
1830 hrs

General-Admiral von Friedeburg,
C-in-C German Navy

General Kinzel, Chief of Staff
to Field-Marshal Busch

Rear-Admiral Wagner, staff officer

Colonel Pollek, staff officer

Major Freidel, staff officer

The belief in the possibility of a short decisive war appears to be one of the most ancient and dangerous of human illusions.

***Robert Lynd*** *(1879-1949), Irish writer under pseudonym Yys (wise). Fervent nationalist. Fluent Gaelic*

Leadership consists of nothing but taking responsibility for everything that goes wrong and giving your subordinates credit for everything that goes well.

***Dwight 'Ike' Eisenhower*** *(1890-1969), American general, statesman. 34th President of the United States*

Older men declare war. But it is youth that must fight and die.

***Herbert Hoover*** *(1874-1964), American engineer, 31st President of United States*

# 14 | Old Age and Death

Whoever saw old age that did not applaud the past and condemn the present?

***Michel de Montaigne** (1533-1592), French philosopher, statesman, author. Fluent in Latin, Greek, Spanish and French*

*Abraham Lincoln's letter to a mother. 1860:*

Dear Madam,

I have been shown in the files of the War Department a statement of the Adjutant-General of Massachusetts that you are the mother of five sons who have died gloriously on the field of battle.

I feel how weak and fruitless must be any words of mine which should attempt to beguile you from the grief of a loss so over-whelming; but I cannot refrain from tendering to you the consolation that may be found in the thanks of the Republic they died to save.

I pray that our heavenly Father may assuage the anguish of your bereavement, and leave you only the cherished memory of the loved and lost, and the solemn pride that must be yours to have laid so costly a sacrifice on the altar of freedom.

Yours very sincerely and respectfully,
***Abraham Lincoln***

Africans drink very little red wine and suffer fewer heart attacks than the British or Americans.

Italians drink large amounts of red wine and suffer fewer heart attacks than the British or Americans.

Germans drink a lot of beer and eat lots of sausages and fats and suffer fewer heart attacks than the British or Americans.

Conclusion: Eat and drink what you like. Speaking English is apparently what kills you.

I'm ninety-five. I still chase girls but I can't remember why.

***George Burns** (born Nathan Birnbaum) (1896-1966), American comedian, actor and writer*

I don't believe in afterlife, although I am bringing a change of underwear.

***'Woody' Allen** (born Allan Konigsberg) (b 1935), American film maker and comedian. Four Academy Awards, 16 nominations*

Admit when you are wrong. The older you get, the more frequently you'll have the opportunity.

***Jennifer Boylan** (born James Boylan) (b 1958), American transgender activist. Professor at Columbia University*

The water's murmur is the voice of my father's father.

***Chief Seattle** (1786-1866), Suquamish chief. Seattle named after him*

Please do not ask
If I am now recovering
Or if I see the light
At the tunnel's end.
Nor speak about relief – or burdens lifted.
And, worst of all, new starts.
Please, please don't ask
If I am getting through –
Have come to terms
Or find my life
Is back on track.
Of course I live each day to each
And gladly smile
My coping, to 'prepare a face
To meet the faces that you meet'.
What else is there to do?
In any case, you would not want to know
The daily loss that lasts eternally.
Just, please, don't ask.

***Frances Gibb**, Legal Editor of 'The Times' 1999-2019.*
*After the death of her husband*

Death is a long journey and you can't take anything to read on it.

***Drue Heinz** (1915-2018), American/English actress and philanthropist. Founder of Hawthornden Prize for literature*

Time is our chequer-board of dark and bright
With peace and turmoil, grieving and delight;
And in the end there's no more time to tell
To make amends; so love, and use time well.

*Words from a gravestone at Ilford Manor, Wiltshire*

# 15 | Epitaphs and Tributes

*At the memorial service of Daniel Macmillan, Viscount Macmillan of Ovenden, there was no address on his instructions that* 'One can't hear them, they never tell the truth and if they did, it shouldn't have been told'.

It is almost impossible to bear the torch of truth through a crowd without singeing somebody's beard.

***Georg Lichtenberg** (1742-1799), German physicist and satirist*

If you have a garden and a library, you have everything you need.

***Marcus Cicero** (106-43 BC), Roman lawyer, statesman and orator. Cicero is Latin for chickpea*

The feathered arrow of an epigram has sometimes been wet with the heart's blood of its victim.

***Isaac d'Israeli** (1766-1848), writer and scholar. Father of Benjamin Disraeli*

Be aware that a halo has to fall only a few inches to be a noose.

***Sir Donald McKinnon** (b 1939), Deputy Prime Minister of New Zealand*

*The Kohima Epitaph is carved on the Memorial of the 2nd British Division in the cemetery of Kohima (North-East India). It reads:*

When you go home, tell them of us and say,
For your tomorrow, we gave our today.

*The verse is attributed to* ***John Maxwell Edmonds*** *(1875-1958), and is thought to have been inspired by the epitaph written by Simonides to honour the Greeks who fell at the Battle of Thermopylae in 480BC*

The type of man who will end up dying in his own arms.

*About Warren Beatty (b 1937), American actor and film producer. Nominated for 15 Academy Awards and 18 Golden Globes*

In memory of Maggie
Who in her time kicked
Two colonels, four majors,
Ten captains, twenty-four lieutenants,
forty-two sergeants,
Four hundred and thirty-two other ranks
AND one Mills bomb

*Epitaph to an army mule, buried in France*

ψγχησ ιατρειοη γςτορ
[The House for Healing the Soul]

*Inscription over the door to the Library of Thebes at Luxor*

The last frail petal of one of the great red roses of old England falls. And the sword sleeps in the scabbard.

***Sir William Connor*** *(1909-1967), journalist for Daily Mirror under pseudonym 'Cassandra'. On the death of Churchill*

Life is a jest, and all things show it;
I thought so once, and now I know it.

*Epitaph of* ***John Gay*** *(1685-1732), poet and dramatist*

*Ce n'est pas génie, ni gloire, ni amour qui reflète*
*la grandeur de l'âme humaine; c'est bonté.*
[It is not genius, nor glory, nor love that reflects
the greatness of the human soul; it is kindness.]

***Jean-Baptiste Lacordaire*** *(1802-1861), French Dominican monk, political activist and orator*

We will remember not the words of our enemies, but the silence of our friends.

***Martin Luther King Jr*** *(1929-1968), American minister and activist during the Civil Rights Movement of 1955. Assassinated in 1968*

Right is right even if no one is doing it;
wrong is wrong even if everyone is doing it.

***Augustine of Hippo*** *(354-430), Christian bishop of Berber origins. Philosopher and theologian*

I slept and dreamed that life was beauty.
I woke and found that life was duty.

*Lines on the tombstone of the suffragette Charlotte Despard (1844-1939), by the Victorian poet* ***Ellen Sturgis Hooper***

Memories are not shackles, Franklin, they are garlands.

***Alan Bennett*** *(b 1934), actor, author and screenwriter. Scholarship to Oxford and first class degree in history. From 'Forty Years on' (1969)*

At last a good plot.

*Words chosen to be on the gravestone of* ***Kathy Lette*** *(b 1979), Australian author of 'How to Kill Your Husband (and other Handy Household Hints)'*

*O mia patria, si bella e perduta*
[O my country, so lovely and so lost]

***Giuseppe Verdi*** *(1831-1901), organist at six, composer at 12, conductor of Philharmonia at 21, first opera at 25. 29 operas. From Chorus of the Hebrew Slaves, Nabucco.*

# Acknowledgements

Once again, **Lindsay Johnstone** has performed the miracle of conjuring up order from an eclectic selection of pieces of paper, scribbles in several colours and torn bits from newspapers and then typing them out faultlessly all the while making corrections, suggesting dates to be checked, querying absurd entries and in general, brilliantly organising this second volume with the same skill as the first volume.

The flair and artistic abilities of my son **Alex** again have been brought to bear in ensuring an elegant presentation. His professional skills as a graphic designer are evident. Perennially busy and burdened by house hunting and the demands of three young children, he somehow found the time to expertly edit and arrange the setting out of every page.

Leaving Kings School, Canterbury, **Charlie Dunn** read for the Bar and is still a member of Lincolns Inn. Changing direction, a spell in retail was followed by a farm and finally a garden centre in Cumbria. Artist great grandparents were the source of Charlie's love of drawing and not a day passes that he has not put pen to paper. I have valued him as a friend and now as a witty illustrator.

*The text of this book is set in Garamond Classico, a version of the Garamond typeface developed by* **Franko Luin** *(1941-2005), a Slovenian-Italian working in Sweden.*

**Claude Garamond** *(1480-1561), a Parisian craftsman, worked as an engraver of punches. Garamond type has spawned a number of subtle variations but fundamentally it is a Roman, upright, serif style, itself based on typefaces of the previous half century, in particular those of the Venetian printer and publisher* **Aldus Manutius** *(1449-1515) and his punchcutter* **Francesco Griffo** *(1450-1518).*

# Index

Lightning Source UK Ltd.
Milton Keynes UK
UKHW050909190822
407482UK00005B/171